AN ANALYSIS
HERMAN WITSIUS'S

The Economy of the Covenants

*Between God and Man
Comprehending a Complete
Body of Divinity*

 CRO●ƏꙄ

D. Patrick Ramsey

and Joel R. Beeke

REFORMATION HERITAGE BOOKS
Grand Rapids, Michigan 49525
and
CHRISTIAN FOCUS PUBLICATIONS

Christian Focus Publications
Geanies House
Fearn, Ross-shire, IV20 1TW, Scotland
www.christianfocus.com

Reformation Heritage Books
2919 Leonard St., NE
Grand Rapids, MI 49525
616-977-0599/Fax 616-977-0889/e-mail jrbeeke@aol.com
website: www.heritagebooks.org
ISBN# 1-892777-22-3

Printed by Bell & Bain Ltd, Glasgow

Introduction

The Life and Theology of Herman Witsius (1636-1708)

Herman Wits (Latinized as Witsius) was born on February 12, 1636, at Enkhuizen to God-fearing parents who dedicated their firstborn to the Lord. His father, Nicholas Wits (1599-1669), was a man of some renown, having been an elder for more than twenty years, a member of Enkhuizen's city council, and an author of devotional poetry.[1] Witsius's mother, Johanna, was a daughter of Herman Gerard, pastor for thirty years of the Reformed church in Enkhuizen. Herman was named after his grandfather with the prayer that he might emulate his godly example.[2]

Education

Witsius was an avid learner. He began Latin studies at age five. Three years later his uncle, Peter Gerard, noticing the boy's gifts, began to tutor him. By the time Witsius took up theological studies in Utrecht at age 15, he could speak Latin fluently. He could read Greek and Hebrew, and had memorizied numerous Scriptures in their original languages. At Utrecht, he studied Syriac and Arabic under Johannes Leusden and theology under Johannes Hoornbeeck, whom he called "my teacher of undying memory." He also studied under Andreas Essenius, whom he honored as "my father in the Lord,"and Gisbertus Voetius, whom he called "the great Voetius."[3] From Voetius he learned how to wed precise Reformed orthodoxy to heartfelt, experiential piety.[4]

After studying theology and homiletics with Samuel Maresius at Groningen, in 1653 Witsius returned to Utrecht, where he was profoundly influenced by the local pastor, Justus van der Bogaerdt. According to Witsius's later testimony, van der Bogaerdt's preaching and fellowship brought him experientially to understand the difference between theological knowledge gleaned from study and the heavenly wisdom taught by the Holy Spirit through communion with God, love, prayer, and meditation. Witsius wrote that he was born again in "the bosom of the Utrecht church by the living and eternal Word of

The Economy of the Covenants

God." Through this godly pastor's influence, Witsius said, he was preserved "from the pride of science, taught to receive the kingdom of heaven as a little child, led beyond the outer court in which he had previously been inclined to linger, and conducted to the sacred recesses of vital Christianity."[5]

Already as a teenager, Witsius had demonstrated his gifts in public debate. In 1655 he defeated some of the leading debaters at the University of Utrecht by showing that the doctrine of the Trinity could be proven from the writings of ancient Jews. When Witsius thanked the moderator for his assistance, the moderator replied, "You neither had, nor stood in need of, any assistance from me."[6]

In 1656 Witsius passed his final examinations and was declared a candidate for the ministry. Due to the abundance of ministers, he had to wait a year before receiving a pastoral call. During that time he applied to the authorities of the French Church in Dort for a license to preach in French-speaking Reformed churches. Witsius often preached in French at Utrecht, Amsterdam, and elsewhere.

Pastorates

On July 8, 1657, Witsius was ordained into the ministry at Westwoud, where his catechizing of young people bore special fruit. But he also encountered opposition because of the congregation's ignorance of their Reformed heritage. Medieval customs such as praying for the dead were still evident in the people. These problems convinced Witsius early in his ministry of the need for further Reformation among the people. It also prompted him to publish his first book, *'t Bedroefde Nederlant* (The Sorrowing Netherlands).[7]

In 1660, Witsius married Aletta van Borchorn, daughter of a merchant who was an elder in Witsius's church. They were blessed with twenty-four years of marriage. Aletta said she could not tell what was greater—her love or her respect for her husband. The couple had five children—two sons, who died young, and three daughters: Martina, Johanna, and Petronella.

In 1661, Witsius was installed in the church at Wormer—one of Holland's largest churches—where he succeeded in uniting warring factions and training the people in divine knowledge. He and his colleague, Petrus Goddaeus, took turns teaching a doctrinal class on weekday evenings to "defend the truth of our teachings against false doctrines" and to inculcate "the sanctity of our teachings in terms of God-fearing conduct." The class began in private homes, then out-

grew that space and moved to the church. Eventually people had to
stand outside the church due to lack of room.[8]

These class lectures were eventually published in a book titled
Practycke des Christendoms (The Practice of Christianity), to which Witsius appended *Geestelycke Printen van een Onwedergeborenen op syn beste
en een Wedergeborenen op syn slechste* (A Spiritual Picture of the Unregenerate at His Best and the Regenerate at His Worst).

Practycke des Christendoms explains the primary grounds of godliness, while the appended work applies those grounds by teaching
what is laudable in the unregenerate and what is culpable in the regenerate. John Owen said he hoped he could be as consistent as Witsius's unregenerate man at his best and that he would never fall so
deeply as Witsius's regenerate man at his worst.

In his writings, Witsius demonstrates the convictions of the *Nadere
Reformatie* (Dutch Second Reformation or "Further Reformation").
The Dutch Second Reformation was largely a seventeenth-century
movement within the Dutch Reformed churches that zealously strove
for the inner experience of Reformed doctrine and personal sanctification as well as the purification of all spheres of life.[9]

Witsius accepted a call to Goes in 1666, where he labored for two
years. In the preface to *Twist des Heeren met syn Wijngaert* (The Lord's
Controversy with His Vineyard), published in Leeuwarden in 1669,
he said he had labored with much peace in this congregation together
with three colleagues, "two of whom were venerated as fathers, and
the third was loved as a brother." Of these four ministers working together in one congregation, Witsius noted: "We walked together in
fellowship to God's house. We did not only attend each other's services, but also each other's catechism classes and other public services,
so that what one servant of God might have taught yesterday, the others confirmed and recommended to the congregation the next day."
Under the influence of these four ministers, "all sorts of devotional
practices blossomed, piety grew, and the unity of God's people was
enhanced," Witsius wrote.[10]

After serving Goes, Witsius went to his fourth pastoral charge,
Leeuwarden, where he served for seven years (1668-1675). In 1672,
called the "year of miracles" because the Dutch Republic survived the
onslaught of four enemies who had declared war on the Netherlands
(France, England, and the German electorates of Cologne and Mun-
ster), Witsius gained renown for faithful ministry in the midst of cri-
sis. Johannes à Marck, a future colleague, said of Witsius that he knew
of no other minister whose labors were so owned of God.[11]

In 1673 Witsius again teamed up with a renowned colleague—this time, Wilhelmus à Brakel, with whom he served two years. At Leeuwarden, Witsius played a critical role mediating disputes between Voetius and Maresius.

Professorships

In 1675, Witsius was called to be a professor of theology. He served in this capacity for the rest of his life, first at Franeker (1675-1680), then at Utrecht (1680-1698), and finally at Leiden (1698-1707).

Shortly after his arrival at Franeker, the university there awarded Witsius a doctorate in theology. His inaugural address, *On the character of a true theologian* (1675), which was attended by scholars from all over the province, stressed the difference between a theologian who knows his subject only scholastically and a theologian who knows his subject experientially.[12]

Under Witsius's leadership the university began to flourish as a place to study theology, especially after the arrival of the 21-year-old professor, Johannes à Marck, in 1678. It soon attracted students from all over Europe.

During his professorship at Franeker, tension between the Voetians and the Cocceians escalated. Gisbertus Voetius (1589-1676), a renowned Reformed scholastic theologian and professor at Utrecht, represents the mature fruit of the *Nadere Reformatie*, much as John Owen does for English Puritanism. Voetius unceasingly opposed Johannes Cocceius (1603-1669), the Bremen-born theologian who taught at Franeker and Leiden, and whose covenant theology, in Voetius's opinion, overemphasized the historical and contextual character of specific ages. Voetius believed that Cocceius's new approach to the Scriptures would undermine both Reformed dogmatics and practical Christianity. For Voetius, Cocceius's devaluing of practical Christianity culminated in his rejection of the Sabbath as a ceremonial yoke no longer binding on Christians. The Voetian-Cocceian controversy racked the Dutch Reformed Church until long after the death of both divines, splitting theological faculties into factions. Eventually both factions compromised, agreeing in many cities to rotate their pastors between Voetians and Cocceians.[13]

Witsius's concern about this controversy moved him to publish *De Oeconomia Foederum Dei cum Hominibus* (1677), first printed in English in 1736 as *The Oeconomy of the Covenants between God and Man, comprehending a Complete Body of Divinity*. It was reprinted numerous times, most recently in two volumes by the den Dulk Christian Foundation in 1990. In governing his systematic theology by the concept of covenant, Witsius uses Cocceian methods while maintaining essentially Voetian theology.

In his work on the covenants, Witsius argued against Roman Catholicism, Arminianism, Socinianism, and those Dutch Protestant theologians, who, with Hugo Grotius, had exchanged a *sola scriptura* theology for an institutionalized, sacramental view of the church based on traditions that paved the way back to Rome. Witsius opposed Grotians "who spoke of a 'law' which was not the law of Moses, a 'satisfaction' which was not through punishment and a 'substitution' which was not of necessity and not vicarious."[14]

Witsius next went to Utrecht, where he labored for eighteen years as professor and pastor. Students from all over the Protestant world attended his lectures; magistrates attended his sermons. On two occasions, his colleagues honored him with the headship of the university (1686, 1697).

In 1685, the Dutch Parliament appointed Witsius as a delegate to represent the Dutch government at the coronation of James II and to serve as chaplain to the Netherlands Embassy in London.[15] While there he met the archbishop of Canterbury as well as several leading theologians. He studied Puritan theology and enhanced his stature in England as a peacemaker. Later, the English church called on him to serve as a mediating figure between antinomians and neonomians— the former accusing the latter of overemphasizing the law, the latter accusing the former of minimizing the law. Out of this came his *Conciliatory Animadversions*, a treatise on the antinomian controversy in England. In this treatise, Witsius argued that God's starting point in His eternal decrees did not demean His activity in time. He also helped facilitate the translation into Dutch of some of the works of Thomas Goodwin, William Cave, and Thomas Gataker and wrote prefaces for them.[16]

Witsius's years at Utrecht were not free from strife. He felt obliged to oppose the theology of Professor Herman A. Roell, who advocated a unique mixture of the biblical theology of Johannes Cocceius and the rationalistic philosophy of René Descartes. Witsius felt that this combination threatened the authority of Scripture. Witsius taught the superiority of faith over reason to protect the purity of Scripture. Reason lost its purity in the fall, he said. Though reason is a critical faculty, it remains imperfect, even in the regenerate. It is not an autonomous judge, but a servant of faith.

Clearly Witsius's understanding of who God is affected his understanding of how we know what we know and that Scripture is the final standard of truth rather than our reason. His knowledge of God through the Scriptures shaped all his thinking. How evident this is in his defense of the penal substitution of Christ against the rationalist Socinus.[17]

Subsequently, Witsius opposed rationalism in the teachings of Balthasar Bekker as well as the popular, separatistic ideas of Jean de Labadie. He admitted that the Reformed churches were seriously flawed, but he strongly opposed separating from the church.

At Utrecht, Witsius published three volumes of *Exercitationes Sacrae* (Sacred Exercises), two on the Apostles' Creed (1681) and one on the Lord's Prayer (1689). Second in importance only to his *Economy of the Covenants*, these books stress the truths of the gospel in a pure, clear manner. The three works birthed in a seminary setting are known as Witsius's trilogy.

In the midst of his busy years at Utrecht (1684), Witsius's wife died. His daughter Petronella, who never married, remained with her father, faithfully caring for him through twenty-four years as a widower.

When he was 62 years old, Witsius accepted a call to serve at the university at Leiden as professor. His inaugural address was on "the modest theologian." At Leiden he trained men from Europe, Great Britain, and America, including several native Americans who had been converted through the work of John Eliot (1604-90).[18]

Within a year (1699), Holland and West Friesland appointed Witsius inspector of the University's theological college. It was a position he held until he retired in 1707 because of ill health. In his last six years he suffered painful bouts of gout, dizziness, and memory lapses.[19] After a serious attack in October 1708, he told friends that his homecoming was near. Four days later, he died at the age of 72, after nearly fifty-two years of ministry. During his last hour, he told his close friend, Johannes à Marck, that he was persevering in the faith that he had long enjoyed in Christ.

All his life Witsius was a humble biblical and systematic theologian, dependent on the Scriptures. He was also a faithful preacher. For him, Christ—in the university, on the pulpit, and in daily living—took preeminence. "Free and sovereign grace, reigning through the person and righteousness of the great Immanuel, he cordially regarded at once as the source of all our hope, and the grand incitement to a holy practice," Fraser wrote of Witsius.[20]

Despite all his learning, Witsius remained concerned about the soundness and piety of the church. All his writing and learning was employed to promote the church's well-being. After his death, his writings were collected in six volumes. We shall briefly look at Witsius's most influential books.

Twist des Heeren (The Lord's Controversy)

In *Twist des Heeren* (1669), Witsius calls for "a holy reformation." Basing his work on Isaiah 5:4, Witsius equates the Netherlands with a second Canaan. Just as God cared for Israel as a vinedresser by providing numerous means of grace, but Israel responded with the wild grapes (Dutch: *stinkende druiven*, "stinking grapes") of sinful indulgence rather than the good grapes of gratitude, so God still expends much care upon His people and His church in the Netherlands despite people's sinful response.

God had led 100,000 Reformed Dutch forebears out of bondage to the tyranny of the papacy and the fury of the Spaniards and planted them as a noble vine. The axe of the Inquisition could not destroy that vine, for God Himself protected the Dutch churches. He granted them peace, edified and multiplied them, and enabled them to walk in the fear of the Lord and the comfort of the Holy Ghost. The Synod of Dort dethroned heresy and enthroned truth. Preachers "eloquent and mighty in the Scriptures" as Apollos (Acts 18:23-24) were given to the churches, though they were now rare in the land, Witsius said.

Shouldn't God expect good grapes from the Dutch churches? If not, where could vital, spiritual godliness be found? Only a few clusters of the grapes of Canaan could be seen. Witsius, like Willem Teellinck before him, complained that "the first love" of the Reformation had largely dissipated due to the the lack of Spirit-empowered preaching, lack of godliness, and lack of church discipline. Instead, novel, dangerous opinions were beginning to grow on God's vine, Witsius said. Those opinions included facets of Descartes' philosophy that promoted reason as the interpreter of Scripture, Cocceius's view of the Lord's Day, which viewed the fourth commandment as ceremonial for the Israelites rather than moral for all ages, and a host of other erroneous innovations.[21]

Another Reformation was needed, Witsius said. The sixteenth-century Reformation did not go far enough because of the disobedience, worldliness, and hard-heartedness of the people. "What a blot it is on the Reformation that we Reformed remain so deformed in our lives," Witsius wrote.[22] Through natural disasters, wars, and quarrels—even among ministers—God was declaring that a new Reformation must begin.

A second Reformation called for the renewal of genuine piety and the abandoning of unrighteousness. Promoting a kind of theocratic idealism, Witsius said that rulers should lead their subjects by renewing their covenant with the Lord. Ministers in particular should live a God-fearing life. They could not reform people until they had reformed themselves, their consciences, conduct, company, and homes. Everyone must examine themselves, repent of sin, and return to the Lord, using God's Word as their guide for life. Witsius wrote, "I plead with you, readers, to turn yourselves sincerely to the Lord.... Begin that holy reformation of your unholy life, which has long been urged upon you, but which, until now, you have obstinately postponed. Begin that reformation now, this very hour. Today, if you hear the Lord's voice, harden not your heart."[23]

Personal reformation begins with an experiential knowledge of sin, self, and God, Witsius explained. The spiritually minded will find rest only in Jesus Christ. The truly pious love God more than themselves, His honor more than their own salvation. They yearn to please God and surrender themselves to God. They see their own sinfulness, and, in light of divine holiness, come to view themselves as less than nothing. They seek to hide themselves behind Christ so that God may view them only through Christ. They want grace to live only for God so they can say with Paul, "I live, yet not I, but Christ liveth in me" (Gal. 2:20).

Such people radiate Christ. The mind in them was also in Christ Jesus (Phil. 2:5). A renewed believer conducts himself like a "little Christ" on earth. He sees Christ in others and loves others in Christ. His life radiates the holiness and glory of God.

Few people in the Netherlands believe such experiential truth, Witsius laments. Christianity is far below the norm. Few die to their own righteousness, live to the glory of Christ, and show sincere love to the brethren.

Witsius taught that only a renewed Reformation could keep the faltering state and church from destroying themselves. Only when purity of doctrine was accompanied by purity of life could the state and church expect God's blessing. Then God would approve the good grapes, and not complain of the wild grapes the Netherlands brought forth.

Economy of the Covenants
Witsius wrote his *magnum opus* on the covenants to promote peace among Dutch theologians who were divided on covenant theology.

Witsius sought to be a theologian of synthesis, who strove to lessen tension between the Voetians and the Cocceians. He wrote in his introduction that "the enemies of our church...secretly rejoice that there are as many and as warm disputes amongst ourselves, as with them. And this, not very secretly neither: for they do not, nor will ever cease to cast this reproach upon us; which, I grieve to say is not so easily wiped away. O! how much better would it be to use our utmost endeavours, to lessen, make up, and, if it could be, put an end to all controversy!"[24]

Economy of the Covenants is not a complete systematic theology, though its title claims that it comprehends "a complete body of divinity." Several major doctrines not addressed here, such as Trinity, creation, and providence, were dealt with later in Witsius's exposition of the Apostles' Creed.

For Witsius, the doctrine of the covenants is the best way of reading Scripture. The covenants are for him what J. I. Packer calls "a successful hermeneutic," or a consistent interpretative procedure yielding a proper understanding of Scripture, both law and gospel.[25] Witsius's work is divided into four books:

- Book I: The Covenant of Works (120 pages)
- Book II: The Covenant of Redemption, or The Covenant of Grace from Eternity Between the Father and the Son (118 pages)
- Book III: The Covenant of Grace in Time (295 pages)
- Book IV: Covenant Ordinances Thoughout the Scriptures (356 pages)

Throughout his exposition of covenant theology, Witsius corrected inadequacies of the Cocceians and infused Voetian content. He treated each topic analytically, drawing from other Reformed and Puritan systematicians to move the reader to clarity of mind, warmth of heart, and godliness of life.

In Book I, Witsius discusses divine covenants in general, focusing on etymological and exegetical considerations related to them (*bĕrîth* and *diathēkē*). He notes promise, oath, pledge, and command as well as a mutual pact that combines promise and law. He concludes that covenant, in its proper sense, "signifies a mutual agreement between parties with respect to something."[26] Then he defined covenant as "an agreement between God and man, about the method of obtaining ultimate blessedness, with the addition of a threat of eternal destruction, against anyone contemptuous of this blessedness."[27] The essence of the covenant, then, is the relationship of love between God and man.

Covenants between God and man are essentially monopleuric (one-sided) covenants in the sense that they can only be initiated by God and are grounded in "the utmost majesty of the most high God." Though initiated by God, these covenants call for human consent to the covenant, to exercise the responsibility of obedience within it and to acquiesce in punishment in case of violation. In the covenant of works, that responsibility is partly gracious and partly meritorious, whereas in the covenant of grace, it is wholly gracious in response to God's election and Christ's fulfillment of all conditions of the covenant.[28]

Nevertheless, all covenants between God and man are dipleuric (two-sided) in administration. Both aspects are important. Without the monopleuric emphasis on God's part, covenant initiation and fulfillment would not be by grace alone; without the dipleuric emphasis of divine initiation and human responsibility, man would be passive in covenant administration. The attempt made by contemporary scholars to force seventeenth-century federal theologians into either a monopleuric or dipleuric concept of the covenant misses the mark, as Richard Muller has shown, both with Witsius as well as his popular, younger contemporary Wilhelmus à Brakel (1635-1711), whose *De Redelijke Godsdienst* (*The Christian's Reasonable Service*) was first printed in Dutch in 1700.[29] Muller concludes, "It is not the case, as some have argued that covenant language cuts against election and grace and that covenant doctrine either relaxes the strict doctrine of the decrees or is itself rigidified by contact with the doctrine of predestination during the scholastic era of Reformed theology."[30]

According to Witsius, the covenant of works consists of the contracting parties (God and Adam), the law or condition (perfect obedience), the promises (eternal life in heaven for unqualified veneration to divine law), the penal sanction (death), and the sacraments (Paradise, the tree of life, the tree of knowledge of good and evil, the Sabbath).[31] Throughout, Witsius stressed the relationship of the covenant of parties in terms of the Reformed concept of covenant. Denying the covenant of works causes serious Christological and soteriological errors, he said.[32]

For example, the violation of the covenant of works by Adam and Eve rendered the promises of the covenant inaccessible to their descendants. Those promises were abrogated by God, who cannot lower His standard of law by recasting the covenant of works to account for fallen man's unrighteousness. Divine abrogation, however, does not annul the demand of God for perfect obedience. Rather, because of the stability of God's promise and His law, the covenant of grace is made effective in Christ, the perfect Law-fulfiller. In fulfilling all the conditions of the covenant of grace, Christ fulfilled all the conditions of the covenant of works. Thus "the covenant of grace is not the abolition, but rather the confirmation of the covenant of works, inasmuch as the Mediator has fulfilled all the conditions of that covenant, so that all believers may be justified and saved according to the covenant of works, to which satisfaction was made by the Mediator," Witsius wrote.[33]

Witsius outlined the relationship of the covenant of works to the covenant of grace in his second book. He discussed the covenant of grace from eternity, or, the covenant of redemption as the *pactum salutis* beteen God the Father and God the Son.[34] In the eternal *pactum*, the Father solicited from the Son acts of obedience for the elect, while pledging ownership of the elect to the Son. This "agreement between God and the Mediator" makes possible the covenant of grace between God and His elect. The covenant of grace "presupposes" the covenant of grace from eternity and "is founded upon it," Witsius said.[35]

The covenant of redemption established God's remedy for the problem of sin. The covenant of redemption is the answer for the covenant of works abrogated by sin. The Son binds Himself to work out that answer by fulfilling the promises and conditions and bearing the penalties of the covenant on behalf of the elect. Ratified by the covenant of redemption, "conditions are offered to which eternal salvation is annexed; conditions not to be performed again by us, which might throw the mind into despondency; but by him, who would not part with his life, before he had truly said, 'It is finished,'" Witsius explained.[36]

This covenant of grace worked out in time (Book 3) is the core of Witsius's work, and covers the entire field of soteriology. By treating the *ordo salutis* within the framework of the covenant of grace, Witsius asserted that former presentations of covenant doctrine were superior to newer ones. He showed how covenant theology binds theologians together rather than drives them apart.

Election is the backdrop of the covenant. Election, as the decree or counsel of God, is God's unilateral, unchangeable resolve that does not depend on human conditions. Here the covenant of grace parts ways with the covenant of works. In the covenant of works, God promised man life on the condition of complete obedience without promising that He would work that obedience in man. In the covenant of grace, God promised to give everything to the elect—eternal life and the means to it: faith, repentance, sanctification, and perseverance. Every condition of salvation is included in God's promises to His elect. Faith is not, properly speaking, a condition, but the way and means through which believers receive the promises of eternal life.[37]

Though the "*internal*, mystical, and spiritual *communion*" of the covenant is established within the elect, there is also an external economy or administration of the covenant. Those who are baptized and raised with the means of grace are in the covenant externally, though many of them "are not in the testament of God" in terms of being saved.[38]

Effectual calling is the first fruit of election, which in turn works regeneration. Regeneration is the infusion of new life in the spiritually dead person. Thus the incorruptible seed of the Word is made fruitful by the Spirit's power. Witsius argued that so-called "preparations" to regeneration, such as breaking of the will, serious consideration of the law and conviction of sin, fear of hell and despairing of salvation, are fruits of regeneration rather than preparations when the Spirit uses them to lead sinners to Christ.[39]

The first act of this new life is faith. Faith, in turn, produces various acts: (1) knowing Christ, (2) assenting to the gospel, (3) loving the truth, (4) hungering and thirsting after Christ, (5) receiving Christ for salvation, (6) reclining upon Christ, (7) receiving Christ as Lord, and (8) appropriating the promises of the gospel. The first three acts are called preceding acts; the next three, essential acts; the last two, following acts.[40]

In the last two acts, the believer promises to live in the obedience of faith and obtains assurance through the reflective act of faith which reasons syllogistically like this: "[Major premise:] Christ offers himself as a full and complete Saviour to all who are weary, hungry, thirsty, to all who receive him, and are ready to give themselves up to him. [Minor premise:] But I am weary, hungry, etc. [Conclusion:] Therefore Christ has offered himself to me, is now become mine, and I his, nor shall any thing ever separate me from his love."[41]

Witsius referred to this conclusion of faith, later called the practical or mystical syllogism, whenever he discussed assurance of faith. In this, he followed Puritan and Dutch Second Reformation thinking.[42] Aware of the dangers of relying upon personal sanctification for assurance—particularly the objections of the antinomians that syllogisms can provide no sure comfort and may lead to "free-will" thinking, Witsius took pains to keep the syllogism within the confines of the doctrines of grace. Like the Puritans, he taught that the syllogism is bound to the Scriptures, flows out of Jesus Christ, and is ratified by the Holy Spirit. The Spirit witnesses to the believer's spirit, not only by direct testimony from the Word, but also by stirring up the believer to observe scriptural marks of grace in his own soul and in the fruits of his life. Those marks of grace lead to Jesus Christ. The syllogism is always scriptural, christological, and pneumatological.

For Witsius, assurance by syllogism is more common than assurance by the direct testimony of the Spirit. Consequently, careful self-examination as to whether one is in the faith and Christ in him is critical (2 Cor. 13:5). If justification issues in sanctification, the believer ought to reason syllogistically from sanctification back to justification—i.e., from the effect to the cause. That is what the apostle John does in his First Epistle General (2:2, 3, 5; 3:14, 19; 5:2).[43]

Witsius is solidly Reformed on justification by faith alone. He speaks of the elect being justified not only in Christ's death and resurrection, but already in the giving of the first gospel promise in Genesis 3:15. Applications of justification to the individual believer occur at his regeneration, in the court of his conscience, in daily communion with God, after death, and on the Judgment Day.[44]

Witsius went on to discuss the immediate results of justification: spiritual peace and the adoption of sonship. These chapters excel in showing the friendship and intimacy between the believer and the Triune God. They place a large measure of responsibility on the believer to be active in preserving spiritual peace and the consciousness of his gracious adoption.[45]

Typical of Puritan and Dutch Second Reformation divines, Witsius devoted the longest chapter in his *ordo salutis* to sanctification. Sanctification is the work of God by which the justified sinner is increasingly "transformed from the turpitude of sin, to the purity of the divine image."[46] Mortification and vivification show the extensiveness of sanctification. Grace, faith, and love are motives for growing in holiness. The goals and means of sanctification are explained in detail. Nevertheless, because believers do not attain perfection in this life, Witsius concluded by examining the doctrine of Perfectionism. God does not grant perfection to us in this life for four reasons: to display the difference between earth and heaven, warfare and triumph, toil and rest; to teach us patience, humility, and sympathy; to teach us that salvation is by grace alone; and to demonstrate the wisdom of God in gradually perfecting us.[47]

After explaining the doctrine of perseverance, Witsius ended his third book with a detailed account of glorification. Glorification begins in this life with the firstfruits of grace: holiness, the vision of God apprehended by faith and an experimental sense of God's goodness, the gracious enjoyment of God, full assurance of faith, and joy unspeakable. It is consummated in the life to come.

The focus of glorification is the enjoyment of God, Witsius said. For example, the joy in the intermediate state is the joy of being with God and Christ, the joy of loving God, and the joy of dwelling in glory.[48]

Book 4 presents covenant theology from the perspective of biblical theology. Witsius offered some aspects of what would later be called progressive redemption, emphasizing the faith of Abraham, the nature of the Mosaic covenant, the role of the law, the sacraments of the Old Testament, and the blessings and defects of the Old Testament. Some of his most fascinating sections deal with the Decalogue as a national covenant with Israel rather than as a formal covenant of works or covenant of grace;[49] his defense of the Old Testament against false charges; his explanation of the ceremonial law's abrogation and the relationship between the covenant of works and the covenant of grace. He then explained the relationship between the testaments and the sacraments of the New Testament era. He strongly supported the restoration of Israel according to Romans 11:25-27.[50] He set Christian liberty in the context of freedom from the tyranny of the devil, the reigning and condemning power of sin, the rigor of the law, the laws of men, things indifferent, and death itself. By including things indifferent, he dispelled the charge that the precisianism of the Puritans and Dutch Second Reformation divines allowed no room for the adiaphora.

In summary, Witsius was one of the first theologians among Dutch Second Reformation divines who drew close ties between the doctrines of election and covenant. He aimed for reconciliation between orthodoxy and federalism, while stressing biblical theology as a proper study in itself.

The Cocceians did not respond kindly to Witsius's efforts to reconcile them and the Voetians. They accused him of extending the covenant of grace back into eternity, thereby helping the Reformed orthodox negate the Cocceian principle of the historical development of redemption.[51]

Witsius's work on covenant theology became a standard work in the Netherlands, Scotland, England, and New England. Throughout this work, he stressed that the motto "the Reformed church needs to be ever reforming" (*ecclesia reformata, semper reformanda*) should be applied to the church's life and not to doctrine since Reformation doctrine was foundational truth. His stress was on experiencing the reality of the covenant with God by faith and on the need for godly, precise living—often called "precisianism" somewhat pejoratively by many historians. Few realize, however, that precisianism avoids the medieval ideal of perfection and the pharisaical ideal of legalism. Witsius's emphasis on precise living is characterized by the following:

- Precisianism emphasizes what God's law emphasizes; the law serves as its standard of holiness.
- Precisianism is accompanied by spiritual liberty, rooted in the love of Christ.
- Precisianism treats others mildly but is strict toward one's self.
- Precisianism focuses primarily on heart motivations and only secondarily on outward actions.
- Precisianism humbles the godly, even as they increase in holiness.
- Precisianism's goal is God's glory.[52]

For Witsius precisianism was essentially the practice of experiential piety, for its core was hidden, heartfelt communion with the faithful covenant-keeping God. In Witsius we have theology that is pious in itself rather than theology to which piety is added. [53]

Witsius emphasized Scripture, faith, experience, and the saving work of the Holy Spirit. Scripture was the norm for all belief. The true believer is a humble student of Scripture, reads Scriptures through the glasses of faith, and subjects all his experiences to the touchstone of Scripture for confirmation. True experience flows from the "star light" of Scripture and the "sunlight" of the Holy Spirit, both of which illumine the soul.[54] These two are inseparable from each other and are both received by faith. Students of Scripture are also students of the Holy Spirit.[55] They experience in the Spirit's heavenly academy the forgiveness of sin, adoption as sons, intimate communion with God, love of God poured into the soul, hidden manna, the kisses of Jesus' mouth, and the assurance of blessedness in Christ. The Spirit leads His pupils to feast with God and to know in His banqueting house that His banner over them is love.[56]

The Apostles' Creed and *The Lord's Prayer*

More than a century after Witsius's death, two of his most significant works were translated into English: *Sacred Dissertations on what is commonly called The Apostles' Creed*, translated by Donald Fraser, 2 vols. (Glasgow, 1823), and *Sacred Dissertations on the Lord's Prayer*, translated by Rev. William Pringle (Edinburgh, 1839). Both of these works are judicious, practical, pointed, and edifying. They are meat for the soul.

Witsius's two-volume work on the Apostles' Creed, originally published in Latin at Franeker in 1681, grew out of lectures he gave to his students at the University of Franeker on what he called "the principal articles of our religion." These lectures affirmed Witsius's maxim: "He alone is a true theologian who adds the practical to the threoretical part of religion." Like all of Witsius's writings, these volumes combine profound intellect with spiritual passion.[57]

Witsius's exposition begins with studies that discuss the title, authorship, and authority of the creed; the role of fundamental articles; and the nature of saving faith. The creed's authority is great but not supreme, Witsius said. It contains fundamental articles that are limited to those truths "without which neither faith nor repentance can exist"and "to the rejection of which God has annexed a threatening of destructions." It is scarcely possible to determine the number of fundamental articles. Some are not contained in the creed but are taken up in lengthier doctrinal standards.[58]

Witsius again addressed the acts of saving faith, affirming that the "principal act" of faith is the "receiving of Christ for justification, sanctification, and complete salvation." He stressed that faith receives "a whole Christ," and that "he cannot be a Saviour, unless he be also a Lord."[59] He reasserted the validity of obtaining assurance of faith by syllogistic conclusions and distinguished temporary faith from saving faith. Because temporary faith can remain until the end of a person's life, Witsius preferred to call it presumptuous faith. These kinds of faith differ in their knowledge of the truth, their application of the gospel, their joy, and their fruits.[60]

The remainder of the work follows a phrase-by-phrase 800-page exposition of the creed, accompanied by more than 200 pages of notes added by the translator. Throughout, Witsius excels in exegesis, remains faithful to Reformed dogmatics without becoming overly scholastic, applies every article of the creed to the believer's soul, and, when occasion warrants, exposes various heresies. His closing chapter on life everlasting is perhaps the most sublime. His concluding applications summarize his approach:

- From this sublime doctrine, let us learn the Divine origin of the Gospel
- Let us carefully inquire whether we ourselves have a solid hope of this glorious felicity
- Let us labor diligently, lest we come short of it

- Let us comfort ourselves with the hope of it amidst all our adversities
- Let us walk worthy of it by leading a heavenly life in this world.[61]

Like Witsius's work on the Apostles' Creed, *Sacred Dissertations on the Lord's Prayer* was based on lectures delivered to his theological students. As such, it is a bit heavy with Hebrew and Greek words; however, Pringle's translation includes a rendering of most words of the original languages into English.

The Lord's Prayer contains more than its title reveals. In his preface to a 230-page exposition of the Lord's Prayer, Witsius devoted 150 pages to the subject of prayer: "First, to explain what is prayer; next, in what our obligation to it consists; and lastly, in what manner it ought to be performed."[62] Though parts of this introduction seem a bit dated (especially chapter 4), most of it is practical and insightful. For example, Witsius's dissertation "On the Preparation of the Mind for Right Prayer" contains valuable guidance on a subject seldom addressed today.

Throughout this introduction, Witsius established that genuine prayer is the pulse of the renewed soul. The constancy of its beat is the test of spiritual life. For Witsius, prayer is rightly deemed, in the words of John Bunyan, "a shield to the soul, a sacrifice to God, and a scourge for Satan."

Witsius stressed the two-part channel of prayer: those who would have God hear them when they pray must hear Him when He speaks. Prayer and work must both be engaged in. To pray without working is to mock God; to work without praying is to rob Him of His glory.

Witsius's exposition of the individual petitions of the Lord's Prayer is a masterpiece. In many instances, the questions receive greater instruction from Witsius's pen than anyone else to date. For example, where else can such insight be found on whether the infant believer and the unregenerate should use the name Father in addressing God?[63]

Gifts and Influence

Witsius had many gifts, as even this outline of *Economy of the Covenants* reveals. As an exegete, he exhibited scriptural simplicity and precision, though at times he leaned toward questionable typological and mystical interpretations.[64] As a historian, he measured movements against the ideal, apostolic church, bringing history and theology from numerous sources to bear upon his reasoning. As a theologian, he grounded spiritual life in regeneration and covenantally applied the entire *ordo salutis* to practical, experiential living. As an ethicist, he set forth Christ as the perfect example in probing the heart and guiding the believer in his walk of life. As a polemicist, he opposed Cartesianism, Labadism, antinomianism, neonomianism, and the excesses of Cocceianism. As a homiletician, he, like William Perkins, stressed the marks of grace to encourage believers and convict nominal Christians.[65]

Throughout his life as pastor and professor, Witsius mediated disputes. Formally a Cocceian and materially a Voetian, he managed to remain friends with both sides. His motto was: "In essentials, unity; in non-essentials, liberty; in all things, prudence and charity." He was noted for meekness and patience and stressed that, despite the church's condition, a believer had no right to separate from the church. One biographer wrote of Witsius: "With him it was a fundamental maxim, that Christ 'in all things must have the preeminence'; and free and sovereign grace, reigning through the person and righteousness of the great Immanuel, he cordially regarded as at once the source of all our hope, and the grand incitement to a holy practice."[66]

Witsius influenced many theologians in his lifetime: Campegius Vitringa and Bernardus Smytegelt in the Netherlands; Friedrich Lampe in Germany; Thomas Boston and the Erskine brothers (Ralph and Ebenezer) in Scotland. James Hervey commended him as "a most excellent author, all of whose works have such a delicacy of composition, and such a sweet savour of holiness, [like] the golden pot which had manna, and was outwardly bright with burnished gold, inwardly rich with heavenly food." John Gill described Witsius as "a writer not only eminent for his great talents and particularly solid judgment, rich imagination, and elegance of composition, but for a deep, powerful, and evangelical spirituality, and savour of godliness."[67]

In the nineteenth century, the Free Church of Scotland translated, published, and distributed 1,000 copies of Witsius's *On the character of a true theologian*, free of charge to its divinity students.[68] William Cunningham said in a prefatory note to that work, "He [Witsius] has long been regarded by all competent judges as presenting a very fine and remarkable combination of the highest qualities that constitute a 'true' and consummate theologian—talent, sound judgment, learning, orthodoxy, piety and unction."[69] Witsius's translator, William Pringle, wrote that his writings "are destined to hold an enduring place among the stores of Christian theology. In extensive and profound acquaintance with the doctrines of scripture, powerful defence of the truth against attacks of adversaries, and earnest exhortations to a holy and devout life, he has few equals."[70]

Rabbi John Duncan described Witsius as "perhaps the most tender, spiritually minded and richly evangelical as well as one of the most learned of the Dutch divines of the old school." He said Witsius had special influence upon him. Duncan's biographers stated "that the attraction proved so strong that for some time he could hardly theologize or preach out of that man's groove."[71]

Witsius's influence continues today. "Learned, wise, mighty in the Scriptures, practical and 'experimental,'" J. I. Packer wrote in 1990, "[Witsius] was a man whose work stands comparison for substance and thrust with that of his British contemporary John Owen, and this writer, for one, knows no praise higher than that!"[72] We trust that the influence of Witsius's writings, faciliated by our analysis, will have a God-glorifying influence upon each of us who "take up and read."

Using Our Guide

Our analysis outline of *Economy of the Covenants* can be used as:

• A "Cliff notes" study guide. For beginning Christians, Witsius's writing style may seem a bit ominous. A quick read of our outlined analysis will substantially ease the reading of Witsius.

• A group study guide. Bible study groups often evolve into theology study groups. Assisted by this outline, Witsius's *Economy of the Covenants* would make a great study for budding theologians.

• A quick reference guide. A.A. Hodge's *Outlines* are most helpful for this, but this analysis should be even quicker. For example, it is a handy tool for looking up Witsius's arguments for limited atonement or his discussion on the contrast between the old and new covenants.

Witsius's trilogy is the cream of Reformed theology. Sound biblical exegesis and practical doctrinal substance abound. May God bless their reprints, together with this guide on Witsius's *magnum opus*, in the lives of many, so that Reformed covenant theology, the Apostles' Creed, and the Lord's Prayer acquire a new depth of meaning. Oh, to be more centered upon our covenant LORD Himself—confessing His truth, hallowing His name, longing for the coming of His kingdom, doing His will!

March, 2002

Joel R. Beeke
D. Patrick Ramsey

[1]B. Glasius, ed., *Godgeleerd Nederland: Biographisch Woordenboek van Nederland-sche Godgeleerden* (Leiden: E. J. Brill, 1861), 3:611.

[2]For biographical detail on Witsius, see especially the standard work on his life and thought, J. van Genderen, *Herman Witsius: Bijdrage tot de kennis der gere-formeerde theologie* ('s-Gravenhage: Guido de Bres, 1953), 1-107.

[3]J. van Genderen, "Herman Witsius (1636-1708)," in *De Nadere Reformatie: Beschrijving van haar voornaamste vertegenwoordigers*, ed. Willem van't Spijker ('s-Gravenhage: Boekencentrum, 1986), 193.

[4]Joel R. Beeke, *Gisbertus Voetius: Toward a Reformed Marriage of Knowledge and Piety* (Grand Rapids: Reformation Heritage Books, 1999).

[5]Donald Fraser, "Memoir of Witsius" prefaced to Herman Witsius, *Sacred Dissertations, on what is commonly called the Apostles' Creed*, trans. Donald Fraser (1823; reprint Phillipsburg, N.J.: Presbyterian and Reformed, 1993), 1:xiv.

[6]Erasmus Middleton, *Biographica Evangelica* (London: R. Denham, 1786), 4:158.

[7]The full title is *'t Bedroefde Nederlant, ofte Betooninge van den elendigen toestant onses Vanderlants* (Utrecht, 1659). For a study of this scarce work, see K. Slik, "Het oudste geschrift van Herman Witsius, in NAKG, Nieuwe serie, deel 41 (1956):222-41.

[8]J. van der Haar, "Hermannus Witsius," in *Het blijvende Woord*, ed. J. van der Haar, A. Bergsma, L.M.P. Scholten (Dordrecht: Gereformeerde Bijbelstichting, 1985), 243.

[9]For a summary of the *Nadere Reformatie*, see Joel R. Beeke, *The Quest for Full Assurance: The Legacy of Calvin and His Successors* (Edinburgh: Banner of Truth Trust, 1999), 286-309.

[10]Van der Haar, *Het blijvende Woord*, 244.

[11]Fraser, *Apostles' Creed*, xvii.

[12]Herman Witsius, *On the character of a true theologian*, ed. J. Ligon Duncan, III (Greenville, S.C.: Reformed Academic Press, 1994).

[13]For further study, see Charles McCoy, "The Covenant Theology of Johannes Cocceius" (Ph.D. dissertation, Yale, 1957); idem, "Johannes Cocceius: Federal Theologian," *Scottish Journal of Theology*, 16 (1963):352-70; idem, *History, Humanity, and Federalism in the Theology and Ethics of Johannes Cocceius* (Philadelphia: Center for the Study of Federalism, Temple University, 1980); C. Steenblok, *Gisbertus Voetius: zijn leven en werken*, 2nd ed. (Gouda: Gereformeerde Pers, 1976); idem, *Voetius en de Sabbat* (Hoorn, 1941); Willem van't Spijker, "Gisbertus Voetius (1589-1676)," in *De Nadere Reformatie: Beschrijving van haar voornaamste vertegen-woordigers* ('s-Gravenhage: Boekencentrum, 1986), 49-84.

[14]George M. Ella, *Mountain Movers* (Durham, England: Go Publications, 1999), 157.

[15]John Macleod, *Scottish Theology* (reprint London: Banner of Truth Trust, 1974), 140.

[16]Cornelis Pronk, "The Second Reformation in the Netherlands," *The Messenger* 48 (Apr. 2001), 10.

[17]*The Economy of the Covenants Between God and Man* (1736; reprint Phillipsburg, N.J.: Presbyterian and Reformed, 1990), 1.2.16; 2.5.8.

[18]Ella, *Mountain Movers*, 158.

[19]William Crookshank, biographical preface to Herman Witsius, *Economy of the Covenants*, 1: 39.

[20]Fraser, *Apostles' Creed*, xxvii.

Introduction xxiii

[21]See Thomas Arthur McGahagan, "Cartesianism in the Netherlands, 1639-1676: The New Science and the Calvinist Counter-Reformation" (Ph.D. dissertation, University of Pennsylvania, 1976); H. B. Visser, *Geschiedenis van den Sabbatstrijd onder de Gereformeerden in de Zeventiende Eeuw* (Utrecht: Kemink en Zoon, 1939).

[22]*Twist des Heeren met syn Wijngaert* (Utrecht, 1710), 393.

[23]Cited by Van Genderen, *De Nadere Reformatie*, 200.

[24]*Economy of the Covenants*, 1:22-23.

[25]Ibid., first page of Packer's unnumbered preface.

[26]Ibid., Book 1, Chapter 1, Paragraphs 3-5 [hereafter 1.1.3-5].

[27]Ibid., 1.1.9.

[28]Ibid., 1.1.15; 1.4.

[29]Wilhelmus à Brakel, *The Christian's Reasonable Service*, trans. Bartel Elshout, ed. Joel R. Beeke, 4 vols. (Morgan, Penn.: Soli Deo Gloria, 1992-95).

[30]"The Covenant of Works and the Stability of Divine Law in Seventeenth-Century Reformed Orthodoxy: A Study in the Theology of Herman Witsius and Wilhelmus à Brakel," *Calvin Theological Journal* 29 (1994):86-87.

[31]Stephen Strehle, Calvinism, *Federalism, and Scholasticism: A Study of the Reformed Doctrine of Covenant* (New York: Peter Lang, 1988), 288.

[32]*The Economy of the Covenants*, 1.2.13-15; 1.3.9-10; 1.4.4-7.

[33]Ibid., 1.11.23.

[34]Ibid., 2.2-4.

[35]Ibid., 2.2.1.

[36]Ibid., 2.1.4; cf. Gerald Hamstra, "Membership in the Covenant of Grace," unpublished research paper for Calvin Theological Seminary (1986), 10.

[37]*The Economy of the Covenants*, 3.1-4; 3.8.6.

[38]Ibid., 3.1.5.

[39]Ibid., 3.6.11-15.

[40]Cornelis Graafland, *De Zekerheid van het Geloof: Een onderzoek naar de geloofsbeschouwing van enige vertegenwoordigers van reformatie en nadere reformatie* (Wageningen: H. Veenman & Zonen, 1961), 162-63.

[41]*The Economy of the Covenants*, 3.7.24.

[42]Joel R. Beeke, *Assurance of Faith: Calvin, English Puritanism, and the Dutch Second Reformation* (New York: Peter Lang, 1991), 113-15, 124-26, 159-69, 247-48.

[43]For the views of Calvin and the Puritans on the syllogisms in assurance, see Beeke, *Quest for Full Assurance*, 65-72, 130-42.

[44]*Economy of the Covenants*, 3.8.57-64.

[45]Ibid., 3.9-11.

[46]Ibid., 3.12.11.

[47]Ibid., 3.12.121-24.

[48]Ibid., 3.14.

[49]Here Witsius follows the minority of the seventeenth-century English Puritans, e.g. Samuel Bolton (*True Bounds of Christian Freedom* [Edinburgh: Banner of Truth Trust, 1994], 99) and John Owen (Sinclair Ferguson, *John Owen on the Christian Life* [Edinburgh: Banner of Truth Trust, 1987], 28).

[50]*Economy of the Covenants*, 4.15.7.

[51]Charles Fred Lincoln, "The Development of the Covenant Theory," *Bibliotheca Sacra*, #397 (Jan. 1943):161-62.

[52]Adapted from Van Genderen, *De Nadere Reformatie*, 206.

[53]I. van Dijk, *Gezamenlijke Geschriften* (Groningen, 1972), 1:314.

[54]*Twist des Heeren*, 167.

[55]Witsius, *On the character of a true theologian*, 35-38.

[56]Herman Witsius, *Miscelleanorum Sacrorum tomus alter* (Lugd. Bat., 1736), 671-72.

[57]Sinclair Ferguson, preface to *Apostles' Creed*, iv.

[58]Witsius, *Apostles' Creed*, 1:16-33.

[59]Ibid., 1:49, 51.

[60]Ibid., 1:56-60.

[61]Ibid., 2:xvi, 470-83.

[62]Herman Witsius, *The Lord's Prayer* (1839; reprint Phillipsburg, N.J.: Presbyterian and Reformed, 1994), 1. The following summary is adapted from my preface in this reprint.

[63]Ibid., 168-70.

[64]J. van Genderen shows how Witsius revealed some mystical tendencies in his enthusiasm for speaking about contemplation, ecstasy, and mystical marriage with Christ, which surfaces especially in his exegesis of the Song of Solomon and some of the Psalms (*Herman Witsius*, 119-23, 173-76, 262). See also Witsius's discussion of the "mystery" of the manna (*Economy of the Covenants*, 4.10.48).

[65]Ibid., 261-63.

[66]Fraser, *Apostles' Creed*, xxvii.

[67]Ibid., ii; Thomas K. Ascol, "Preface," *Economy of the Covenants*.

[68]Michael W. Honeycutt, introduction to *On the character of a true theologian*, 7.

[69]Ibid., 19.

[70]*The Lord's Prayer*, frontispiece.

[71]Pronk, "The Second Reformation in the Netherlands," *The Messenger* 48 (Apr. 2001), 10.

[72]*The Economy of the Covenants*, back cover.

An Analysis

of

Witsius's

Economy of the Covenants

Book 1

Chapter 1: Of Divine Covenants in General.
I.   The various uses of *berith* in Scripture.
   A. An immutable ordinance made about a thing; Jer. 33:20.
   B. A sure and stable promise, though not mutual; Ex. 34:10.
   C. A precept; Jer. 34:13-14.
   D. A mutual agreement between parties, with respect to something; Gen. 14:13; 26:28-29; 1 Sam. 18:3.
II. God's covenant with man.
   A. Definition: "A covenant of God with man, is an agreement between God and man, about the way of obtaining consummate happiness; including a commination of eternal destruction, with which the contemner of the happiness, offered in that way, is to be punished."
   B. The three elements of the covenant.
     1. A promise of eternal life.
     2. Prescription of the conditions for obtaining the promise.
     3. Penal sanction against transgressors of the conditions of the Covenant.
   C. The Covenant was not an option for man. [1]
     1. Required by the law of God.
     2. Sovereignty of God over man.
     3. Required by man's love for himself.
     4. Man's conscience knows it is just.
   D. In Scripture, there are two covenants of God with man.
     1. Covenant of Works.
     2. Covenant of Grace.
   E. Similarities between the two covenants.
     1. Contracting parties are the same.
     2. Same promise of eternal life.
     3. The condition of both is the same, i.e. perfect obedience.

---

[1] Witsius writes, "It is not left to man to accept or reject at pleasure God's covenant. Man is commanded to accept it, and to press after the attainment of the promises in the way pointed out by the covenant. Not to desire the promises, is to refuse the goodness of God. To reject the precepts is to refuse the sovereignty and holiness of God; and not to submit to the sanction is to deny God's justice."

    4. The goal of both is the same, i.e. the glory of God.

F. Differences between the two covenants.

    1. The character or relation of God and man is different.

    2. There is a mediator in the covenant of grace.

    3. The condition of the covenant is fulfilled by the mediator in the covenant of grace.

    4. Promise obtained in covenant of works would have been obtained by merit whereas in the covenant of grace it is obtained by grace.

    5. In the covenant of grace the whole of salvation, and all the requisites to it, are absolutely promised whereas in the covenant of works eternal life was conditioned upon man's mutable obedience.

    6. Special end of covenant of works was the justice, holiness and goodness of God whereas it is the grace and mercy of God in the covenant of grace.

Chapter 2: Of the Contracting Parties in the Covenant of Works.

I. The contracting parties of the covenant of works are God and man.

II. Adam sustained a two-fold relation.

    A. As man.

        1. "A rational creature, under the law of God, innocent, created after the divine image and endued with sufficient powers to fulfil all righteousness."

        2. Created perfectly with knowledge, righteousness and holiness.

        3. The whole extent of the image of God consists of three parts.

            a. Antecedently, in that it consists in the spiritual and immortal nature of the soul and in the faculties of understanding and will.

            b. Formally and principally in these endowments or qualities of the soul, viz. righteousness and holiness.

            c. Consequentially, in the immortality of the whole man, and his dominion over the creatures.

    B. As head and root, or representative of mankind.

        1. The whole of history proves this fact as he was the first man to whom was spoken the creation ordinances and mandate.

2. Penal sanction passed onto Adam's posterity; Rom. 5:12.
3. The contrast with the second Adam; Rom. 5:12ff.

III. God is righteous in governing the world in this fashion.
   A. No one would have complained if Adam had obeyed.
   B. No one can say they could have done better.
   C. Everyone has sinned personally.

Chapter 3: Of the Law or Condition of the Covenant of Works.

I. The law of the Covenant is twofold.
   A. The law of nature implanted in Adam.
   B. The symbolic law.

II. The law of nature.
   A. It is the rule of good and evil, inscribed by God on man's conscience, even at his creation, and therefore binding upon him by divine authority.
   B. Law is compatible with love.
      1. Law is not enforcement or coercion but the obligation of a just act based upon the holiness of God.
      2. It is not absurd for a father/son relationship to be governed by laws.
      3. It is not repugnant to do something willingly, naturally and at the same time by law.
      4. Sin or breach of love is transgression of the law.
      5. Law commands us to obey willingly and lovingly.
   C. The law of nature is the same in substance with the decalogue.
   D. The Creator/creature distinction necessitates law.
      1. God would deny Himself.
      2. Man would be autonomous.
   E. The law requires external and internal obedience.
   F. The universal precepts of the law are founded upon the nature of God, that is, an expression of His character.
      1. Otherwise, God who is by nature the highest good does not have to be so esteemed, which is a contradiction.
      2. Otherwise, Christ died in vain for God could have arbitrarily declared sinners to be righteous.

III. The symbolic law.
   A. The symbolic law was the tree of knowledge of good and evil.

B. Two-fold reason for the symbolic law.
  1. With respect to God, to test and try man's obedience.
  2. With respect to man, probatory law with reward of eternal life and punishment of eternal death.
C. Lessons to be learned from the symbolic law.
  1. God is Lord of all things.
  2. Man's true happiness is placed in God alone.
  3. To be satisfied with what God gives us.
  4. To desire the greater good or reward upon obedience.
  5. True happiness is obtained but by obedience.

IV. A perfect three-fold keeping of the law was required.
  A. Of parts with respect to subject and object: The whole man, body and soul, had to keep the whole law.
  B. Of degrees: Man had to keep the law with all diligence and heart.
  C. Of perseverance: Man had to persevere in keeping the law without fault.

Chapter 4: Of the Promises of the Covenant of Works.
I. The Covenant of Works did include promises contrary to the Socinians.
  A. Man's natural conscience teaches him, that God desires not to be served in vain, nor that obedience to his commands will go unrewarded and for nought; Heb. 11:6.
  B. True faith is rooted in the word and promise of God; Rom. 5:17.
  C. The tree of life represented the promise of eternal life.
  D. If no promise had been made, man would have lived without hope and lack of hope is characteristic of the fall; Eph. 2:12.
  E. God's word to Cain, "If thou doest well, shalt thou not be accepted"; Gen. 4:7.
  F. The very threatening infers a promise.

II. The promise made to man was eternal life.
  A. Jesus came to do what the law could not do because man sinned; Rom. 8:3. Jesus came to procure eternal life therefore it was promised to man from the beginning.
  B. The law itself was ordained to life; Rom. 7:10; Gal. 3:21.
  C. Christ, the second Adam, earned eternal life for us.
  D. It is most agreeable to have promises in a covenant.
III. The nature of the promise of eternal life.

A. Foundational truths.
 1. God owes nothing to man. Man cannot merit anything from God.
 2. God cannot punish a holy creature.
 3. God cannot refuse to grant a holy creature the communion of Himself.
B. The promise of the Covenant of works does not pertain to the above for it contained greater things designated "eternal life":
 1. A higher degree of happiness in God.
 2. Confirmation in holiness.
C. Witsius is unsure whether the promise of eternal life springs from God's goodness (i.e. his nature) or good pleasure.

Chapter 5: Of the Penal Sanction.
I. Various observations concerning the penal sanction; Gen. 2:17.
 A. Death is the consequence of sin and therefore not natural.
 B. Sin here expressed is the transgression of the symbolic law.
 C. Punishment for sin is in accord with God's authority and justice.
 D. The term death is used generally to include all its meanings.
 E. Spoken to Adam as the head of mankind.
 F. Penal sanction would be administered immediately.

II. The various meanings of death in Scripture.
 A. Death is the separation of body and soul.
 B. Death means vanity or frustration of this life along with its pain and miseries.
 C. Death means spiritual death.
 D. Death means eternal death of body and soul.

III. The necessity of the penal sanction for sin.
 A. The majesty of God.
 1. God is a jealous God for His own glory and majesty.
 2. God cannot deny Himself, His supreme majesty.
 B. The holiness of God.
 1. A holy God cannot be joined with a sinner without satisfaction made to his justice.
 2. A holy God cannot look upon sin.
 3. A holy God hates sin and the sinner; Deut. 16:6; Ps. 5:4-6.
 4. A holy God cannot be like the sinner by not punishing sin.

     5. God manifests his holiness when he punishes the wicked;
       Lev. 10:3.
  C. The justice of God.
     1. Justice is an essential attribute of God.
     2. God's justice demands sin be punished with death; Rom. 1:32.
  D. God does not delight in the death of the wicked.
     1. Yet in one sense He does rejoice in the death of the
       wicked; Deut. 28:36.
     2. God loves Himself more than man. Thus it is "necessary
       that God should prefer the destruction of his wicked
       creature to that of his own glory, so it is necessary to
       punish the wicked."

IV. The penal sanction of death is based upon the just nature of God.
  A. Eternal death is not an arbitrary sanction.
  B. Sin is infinite in relation to its attack upon God who is infinite
     (and not in an absolute sense since there are degrees of sin),
     therefore punishment must be infinite as well.

Chapter 6: Of the Sacraments of the Covenant of Works.

I. Reasons for the sacraments.
  A. Visible proclamation of the covenant.
  B. Strengthen our faith in God's promise.
  C. A foretaste of eternal blessings.
  D. Remind us of our duty to God.

II. The sacraments of the covenant of works.
  A. Paradise.
  B. The tree of life.
  C. The tree of knowledge of good and evil.
  D. The Sabbath.

III. The sacrament of Paradise.
  A. Paradise signified heaven.
  B. Paradise reminded Adam to be active.

IV. The sacrament of the tree of life signified the Son of God who is
    the source of life in all covenants.

V. The sacrament of the tree of knowledge of good and evil.
  A. Signified the promise of the covenant.
  B. Signified the curse of the covenant.
  C. A memorial of our duty towards God.

Chapter 7: Of the First Sabbath.

I.   The Sabbath began at Creation and not at Mt. Sinai.

II. The nature of the Sabbath.
    A. God rejoiced over His work.
    B. God blessed man.

III. The Sabbath as a sacrament.
    A. God's resting signified His far more glorious rest.
    B. God's resting signified man's eternal rest in God after his probation.

Chapter 8: Of the Violation of the Covenant of Works on the part of Man.

I.   The covenant in its whole constitution was violated by Adam's sin.

II. Observations concerning Satan's temptation.
    A. He doubts God's word.
    B. He doubts or undermines the penalty of sin.
    C. Promises greater happiness.
        1. Adam was promised greater happiness upon obedience.
        2. Satan tempted him to obtain it through disobedience.
        3. Note parallel with Christ's third temptation; Matt. 4:8-11.
    D. Appeals to God as a witness to his lie.

III. Adam's sin was predetermined by God.
    A. Concurrence: For man to act, God has to act. And if God acts then man acts. Man cannot act independently from God. Acts 17:28; Isa. 10:15.
    B. God withholds His morally good influence in sin.
    C. Man was not forced to sin.
    D. God's decree is the foundation for man's liberty.
    E. God is not the author of sin.

IV. The Imputation of original sin; Rom. 5:12.
    A. An actual sin is in view.
    B. "All" includes those who did not personally sin. Therefore Adam's sin was imputed to them.
    C. It is due to Adam's one sin that death came to all.
    D. Analogous to salvation in Christ.
    E. Only one sin of Adam is imputed to his posterity.

Chapter 9: Of the Abrogation of the Covenant of Works on the part of God.

I. Eternal truths that transcend the abrogation of the covenant.
   A. Perfect obedience is (still) required.
   B. Perfect obedience is necessary to obtain eternal life.
   C. Disobedience is punished by death.

II. The Fall did not abrogate the duty to keep the law.
   A. Arminius believed that it did.
      1. Sin broke the covenant therefore obedience not required.
      2. Man has no ability to obey therefore God does not require him to obey.
      3. Can love be required from man who is under the curse of God?
   B. Witsius answers Arminius.
      1. Obligation to obey is founded principally upon God and not a covenant.
         a. The execution of penal sanctions does not abrogate the law.
         b. God does administer greater punishment.
      2. Inability does not negate responsibility to obey.
         a. Man is the cause of his inability.
         b. Man's sin cannot diminish God's authority for that is contrary to God's nature.
         c. To require no obedience is to require obedience.
         d. Arminius' doctrine makes man God.
      3. The law to love God is rooted in His nature.
   C. The law does not change because God does not change.

III. The Gospel did not abrogate the duty to keep the law.
   A. Covenant of grace confirms the covenant of works. Perfect obedience is required to obtain eternal life because Christ's life and death was necessary to redeem his people.
   B. The fruit of Christ's work does not change the law but the sinner.
   C. The law does not change because God does not change.

IV. The abrogation on the part of God was that man can no longer obtain eternal life by the keeping of the law.

Book 2

Chapter 1: Introduction to the Covenant of Grace.
I.   The covenant of grace illustrates God's adorable perfections.

II. Definition: "The covenant of grace is a compact or agreement between God and the elect sinner; God on his part declaring his free good-will concerning eternal salvation, and every thing relative thereto, freely to be given to those in covenant, by, and for the mediator Christ; and man on his part consenting to that good-will by a sincere faith."

Chapter 2: Of the Covenant between God the Father and the Son.
I.   Definition: Father gives the Son to be Head and Redeemer of the elect; and the Son presents himself as a Sponsor or Surety for them.

II. Evidence for the Covenant of Redemption.
   A. Scriptural proof: Luke 22:29; Heb. 7:22; Gal. 3:17; Psa. 119:122; Isa. 38:14; Zech. 6:13.
   B. The economic relationship between the Father and Son, that is Christ calling God Father and God calling Christ servant, points to a covenant of redemption.
   C. The particulars of the Covenant.
      1. Contracting parties: Father and Son.
      2. Proposal by the Father (John 10:18), includes a promise and right to ask for promise upon obedience; Ps. 2:8.
      3. Acceptance of the covenant by the Son; John 14:31.
      4. Performance by the Son; John 19:30.
   D. The baptism of Christ (Matt. 3:16; Luke 3:22), is a sign and seal of the covenant.

Chapter 3: The Nature of the Covenant between the Father and the Son more fully explained.
I.   Time frame of the covenant.
   A. Eternity; 1 Pet. 1:20; Prov. 8:23; Eph. 1:4; John 17:6; Rev. 13:8.
   B. Immediately after the fall.
   C. Time of the Incarnation.

II. Relationship between Christ and the Law.
    A. As God He was subject to no one and nothing.
    B. As man He was subject to moral, ceremonial and civil laws.
    C. As mediator He was subject to earn eternal life and pay our
       debt of sin, i.e., active and passive obedience.
       1. Active subjection to the law.
          a. As a rule of life (involuntary).
          b. As a way to obtain eternal life (voluntary).
       2. Passive obedience consisted of various miseries of body
          and soul from the cradle to the cross (Rom. 8:3; voluntary).
    D. Relationship between two natures of Christ and the law (in
       the sense of earning eternal life and paying the debt of sin).
       1. Divine nature was not truly subject. Divine superiority or
          glory was veiled, i.e., not put on display and thus did not
          hinder the human nature from being truly subject.
       2. Human nature was truly subject.
       3. Active obedience is appropriated to the God-man and not
          just the human nature; necessary for the salvation of
          God's people.
    E. Subordination of Christ with respect to:
       1. Human nature.
       2. Mediatorial office which is an economical subordination.

III. Could the Son withdraw from the Covenant?
    A. As God He could withdraw.
    B. As man He could not withdraw.
       1. The law of love constrained him; 1 John 3:16; John 15:13.
       2. He had promised to do so from all eternity.
       3. God's promises would have been nullified.
       4. It would have been sin to do so and Christ cannot sin.

IV. Relationship between reward and obedience of Christ.
    A. Reward promised is the highest degree of glory.
       1. As a man:
          a. Perfect fruition of God.
          b. Exalted above all creatures.
          c. Glory of God shines through his body.
       2. As God, His glory is unveiled.
       3. As the God-man:
          a. Is highly exalted; Phil. 2:9; Eph. 1:21.
          b. The church is given to Him; Eph. 1:22.

    c. Receives all power; Matt. 28:18.

    d. Gifts for the Church; 1 Cor. 12:12; Eph. 4:8; Acts 2:33.

B. The obedience of Christ merited the reward; Isa. 53:12; Ps. 45:7; Phil. 2:8-9; Heb. 12:2.

Chapter 4: Of the Person of the Surety.

I. The Saviour must be true man, consisting of a soul and body; Heb. 2:10,11,16 17.

II. The Saviour must be a righteous man; Heb. 4:15; Rom. 5:19.

  A. Covenant demands perfect holiness.

  B. Unrighteous man cannot save himself; Jer. 30:21.

  C. Only a righteous man can save others; Heb. 7:26, 9:14; 1 Pet. 1:19.

  D. Virgin birth immunized the Saviour from original sin.

    1. Symbolic view: Virgin birth was a symbol appointed by God whereby he was separated from sinners. The miracle itself had no inherent power to keep the Saviour from original sin.

    2. Literal view: Virgin birth had inherent power to keep the Saviour from original sin because it is possible that part of the body is not under the curse of sin nor a means of transferring guilt.

III. The Saviour must be true God; Isa. 43:11.

  A. Only God can restore to us true liberty. For he who sets us free, makes a purchase of us for his property and possession; 1 Cor. 6:19-20.

  B. Only God can give us eternal life which is Himself.

  C. Only God can give us the right to become sons of God.

  D. The Saviour is worthy of worship; Isa. 45:25; Luke 1:47.

  E. Only God can effect the new creation.

IV. The Saviour must be God-man.

  A. He had to be man in order to obey, submit, and suffer.

  B. He had to be God at the same time in order to have his obedience, submission, and suffering to be of sufficient value for the redemption of the elect.

  C. He had to be God at the same time in order to be able to bear the fierceness of divine wrath and conquer death by his resurrection.

Chapter 5: Of the Suretyship and Satisfaction of Christ.

I. Christ is called our Surety because he made satisfaction to God
    for us.
    A. Socinian definition of satisfaction: Partial satisfaction.
    B. Biblical definition of satisfaction: Complete satisfaction.

II. Christ could, without injury or disgrace to himself, perform the
    satisfaction to God for us.
    A. He was lord of his life; able to lay it down for others, John 10:18.
    B. As God-man he could endure the punishment and perform an
        obedience of such value as to be more than equivalent to the
        obedience of all the elect.
    C. His life and death demonstrated an incomprehensible love
        for God and men.
    D. His taking on human flesh was not injurious to his deity
        since he did not cease from being God.

III. God the Father was able to accept the satisfaction of Christ.
    A. Because it satisfied the character/nature of God.
        1. The truth of God.
        2. The goodness of God.
        3. The justice of God.
        4. The holiness of God.
    B. Because it demonstrated the glory of God.
        1. The all-sufficiency of God.
        2. The perfections of God.

IV. The relationship between the suretyship of Christ and the law.
    A. The law was not abrogated or derogated in any fashion.
        1. The law says that perfect obedience is required for eternal
            life and that every sinner will suffer eternal death.
        2. The law does not state that the perfect righteousness or
            punishment must be performed by the very person to be
            saved.
        3. The law does not state that the punishment must be
            infinite with respect to duration.
    B. The law was fully satisfied by Christ; Rom. 8:4; Isa. 53:2;
        John 8:29, 46.
    C. It was not unjust for Christ to be punished for us.
        1. God can lay the punishment for sin upon Christ; Isa. 53.
        2. Jesus willingly laid down his life for our sins.

3. God determines what is just and not our reason.

V. The relationship between the satisfaction of Christ and the elect.
 A. The obedience of Christ was for our own good.
   1. His miracles demonstrated the truthfulness of his message.
   2. His holy life was an example to us; 1 Pet. 2:21.
   3. His holy life pointed the way to heaven; Heb. 12:14.
 B. The obedience of Christ was performed by him in our stead
    in order that we might receive eternal life; Rom. 5:16-19.
 C. The obedience of Christ was sufficient for all.
   1. His deity enabled his obedience to be of inestimable value.
   2. His humanity enabled him to obey in our place.
 D. The obedience of Christ did not abrogate our responsibility to
    obey the law.
   1. There are two uses of the law to be considered.
     a. The law as the duty of the creature to his Creator.
     b. The law as a means of acquiring eternal life.
   2. Christ fulfilled the second use whereas the first continues
      to be binding upon man.

Chapter 6: What Sufferings of Christ are Satisfactory.
I. All the sufferings of Christ during his humiliation are satisfactory.
 A. The Scripture speaks of the satisfactory sufferings of Christ in
    general terms; Isa. 53:1-7; Heb. 2:10; 5:8-9; 1 Pet. 2:21.
 B. The actual death of Christ is considered part of the satisfaction.
   1. Isa. 53:10; Matt. 20:18; John 10:15; 1 Pet. 3:18; Col. 1:21-22;
      Rom. 5:10; Heb. 9:15; Rom. 8:34.
   2. Typological argument:
     a. The typical satisfaction was effected by the shedding
        of blood of the animal, thereby requiring separation of
        body and soul.
     b. Heb. 10:20. The veil (Christ's body) had to be rent which
        was done when he died.
 C. Christ's physical sufferings (e.g. his scourging) are accounted
    as part of the satisfaction; Isa. 53:5; 1 Pet. 2:24.
 D. Christ's sufferings in the garden of Gethsemane are
    considered part of his satisfaction.
 E. Christ's sufferings would violate the justice of God if they
    were not endured in our place.

II. Arguments against all of Christ's sufferings being satisfactory.
   A. From Scripture:
     1. Zech. 3:9 says that the sin of the whole earth will be removed in one day.
     2. Heb. 9:28; 10:10,12,14 says that the death of Christ on the cross was the expiatory sacrifice by which the elect are perfected.
     3. Christ could not have been a priest until his thirtieth year nor could he have been a sacrifice until the seventh day.
     4. Christ, except for a few hours, was in the favor of God.
   B. From the Apostles' Creed: Christ suffered under Pontius Pilate.
   C. From the Heidelberg Catechism:
     1. Questions #31, 67, 70, 75, 80.
     2. Question # 37 refers to being bound to endure and not actually experiencing the wrath of God.

III. Witsius responds to the arguments.
   A. From Scripture:
     1. The death of Christ was the completion of all of his sufferings.
     2. Christ was always a priest and mediator (Luke 2:49) since his birth though he was not publicly inaugurated until his thirtieth year. Moreover, the year is with reference to Levites and not priests.
     3. Christ's offering was completed on the cross but he was before that the Lamb of God who takes away the sins of the world. Moreover, by their reasoning Christ would have had to die at one year old.
     4. Christ was still the beloved Son of God even while hanging on the cross.
   B. From the Apostles' Creed:
     1. The Creed does not intend to distinguish the satisfactory sufferings from those which are not. Rather the time in which Christ completed his sufferings.
     2. Since they believe only the sufferings on the cross were satisfactory, one would have to exclude the scourging under Pilate.
   C. From the Heidelberg Catechism: they simply misinterpret the catechism.
     1. These questions deal with the completion of Christ's sufferings.

2. Question #37 is plain. To endure is to experience the wrath of God.

Chapter 7: Of the Efficacy of Christ's Satisfaction.
I.   The efficacy of Christ's satisfaction is twofold.
   A.   Christ obtained for himself, as Mediator, a right to all of the elect; Ps. 2:8; Isa. 53:10.
   B.   Christ obtained for the elect an immunity from all misery and a right to eternal life to be applied to them; Matt. 26:28; Gal. 1:4; Tit. 2:14.
      1.   Christ did not achieve a bare possibility of salvation but actual salvation for His elect.
         a.   The idea of redemption, ransom and price of redemption infers the reality and not possibility of salvation.[2]
         b.   Scripture declares that the proximate effect of redemption is actual salvation; Rom. 3:24; Eph. 1:7; Col. 1:14; Heb. 9:12; 1 Cor. 6:20; Acts 20:28; Gal. 4:4-5.
         c.   Scripture does not speak of Christ's death as a possibility of the remission of sins.
         d.   It is absurd to believe that Christ died for one who would eventually be sent to hell.
         e.   Since possibility may never become reality, Christ may never receive the promise given to him by the Father.
      2.   The benefits of salvation are not bestowed upon the elect before effectual calling, faith, repentance, and actual union with Christ.
II. Arminius argues against an actual salvation of God's elect by Christ's death.
   A.   "God has fully right to impart those benefits to whom he thinks proper, and on what conditions he is pleased to prescribe."
   B.   If Christ's death accomplished salvation for the elect then "they are entitled to ask those benefits of God, in right payment and purchase made, *without God's having any right to require of them faith in Christ and conversion to God.*"
   C.   "The righteousness wrought out by Christ is not ours as wrought out, but as imputed to us by faith."

---

[2]Witsius writes, "It is neither customary, nor equitable, that after paying the price, it should remain uncertain, whether the captive is to be set free or not."

III. Witsius answers Arminius.
  A. Answers to the first argument.
    1. God is bound to his promise.
    2. Faith and repentance are part of the blessings (Eph. 1:3) bestowed upon the elect on the merit of Christ's satisfaction.
    3. Faith and repentance are not requisite conditions before some effects of Christ's death are communicated to a person, e.g. regeneration.
  B. Answers to the second argument.
    1. God's elect can boldly ask for blessings because of what Christ has done.
    2. No one can ask for those blessings unless he has first been converted.
    3. God cannot require faith and obedience as the means to earn and right to ask for eternal life. This is based upon the person and work of Christ alone.
  C. Answers to the third argument.
    1. Faith is considered as applying the already accomplished (impetrated) salvation. It is the result of Christ's mediation.
    2. Salvation is ours with respect to right before we are saved and ours by possession when we believe. Otherwise known as passive and active justification.

Chapter 8: Of the Necessity of Christ's Satisfaction.

I. The real issue at stake with regard to this controversy.
  A. The issue is not the absolute power of God.
    1. We must not ask if God by an act of His power could have saved man another way.
    2. For God can do nothing but that which is consistent with his holiness, justice, truth and the rest of his attributes.
  B. The issue is the holiness and justice of God. Was Christ's satisfaction for salvation of the elect owing to the mere good pleasure of God or was it necessary to satisfy the justice and holiness of God?

II. Arguments in favor of the necessity of Christ's satisfaction.
  A. An unnecessary satisfaction is contrary to the goodness, wisdom and holiness of God.

B. An unnecessary satisfaction mitigates against the Scripture's stress on the great love of God as demonstrated in the giving of his Son.

C. Christ's satisfaction was a declaration of the righteousness of God; Rom. 3:25.

D. Animal sacrifices could not atone for sin (Heb. 10:1,4,11); only the sacrifice of Christ could atone for sin.

E. Heb. 10:26 infers that sacrifice is necessary for pardon.

F. The necessary satisfaction of Christ exalts the attributes of God.

G. The necessary satisfaction of Christ promotes Christian piety.

H. The necessary satisfaction of Christ does not derogate any of God's attributes.

Chapter 9: Of the Persons for whom Christ Engaged and Satisfied.

I. Explanation of the doctrine of particular atonement.
   A. Christ's satisfaction was sufficient for all.
   B. Christ, as man, loved all men according to the commandment.
   C. Christ's satisfaction has brought much good even to the reprobate.
   D. The Gospel is freely offered to all without distinction.
   E. Christ only died for the elect.

II. Scriptural support for the doctrine of particular atonement.
   A. The "all" of 2 Cor. 5:15, Heb. 2:9, Col. 1:20, and 1 Tim. 2:6 is restricted to the elect.
   B. The term "world" in such passages as 1 John 2:2 refers to "the collective body of believers or of the elect."
   C. The Scripture says that Christ died for his sheep, his church, his people, and his peculiar people; John 10:15; Acts 20:28; Eph. 5:25; Tit. 2:14.
   D. The accomplishment of Redemption is only as extensive as its application; Tit. 2:14. For the accomplishment necessitates application as is implied in the words "ransom" and "bought."
   E. The use of marriage to describe the relationship between Christ and his church.
   F. The sacrifices in the Old Testament which were a type of the sacrifice of Christ were designed for Israel alone.
   G. The satisfaction of Christ for the reprobate is unworthy of the wisdom, goodness, and justice of God.

Chapter 10: After what manner Christ used the Sacraments.
I. The role of the Sacraments in the life of Christ.
    A. The use of the sacraments was not a matter of choice but a
        duty incumbent upon Christ.
    B. The sacraments were signs and seals of the covenant between
        God the Father and God the Son.
        1. The benefits of salvation for His church were promised to
            Christ.
        2. Christ promised to faithfully redeem the elect.

II. The sacraments which Christ used.
    A. Circumcision.
    B. Baptism.
    C. The Passover.
    D. The Lord's Supper.

Book 3

Chapter 1: Of The Covenant of God with the Elect.

I. The contracting parties of the covenant are God and the Elect.
  A. God is to be considered as:
    1. All sufficient in Himself for sinful man.
    2. Merciful and gracious to sinful man; Ex. 34:6-7.
    3. Just to enter into a relationship with sinners.
    4. Wise to be able to enter a relationship with sinners; Eph. 3:10.
  B. The Elect are to be considered as:
    1. Lost miserable sinners; Tit. 3:4-5.
    2. Chosen by God to grace and glory.
    3. Those for whom Christ died.
  C. The economic roles of the Trinity.
    1. The Father is the principle author of salvation; 2 Cor. 5:19; and appointed the elect to be heirs of himself and co-heirs with his Son; Rom. 8:17.
    2. The Son is the Mediator, Testator and distributor (John 10:28) of all the blessings.
    3. The Spirit applies, signs, and seals the blessings to the elect.
  D. The covenant with the elect is restricted to the invisible, spiritual communion of the covenant.

II. The promises of the covenant.
  A. Salvation itself and the means leading to it are promised; Jer. 31:33.
  B The difference between the promises of the Covenant of Works and Covenant of Grace.
    1. Only eternal life was promised in the Covenant of Works.
    2. Eternal life and the means to receive it are promised in the Covenant of Grace.

III. The conditions of the Covenant of Grace.
  A. Definition of a condition: a condition is that action, which being performed gives a man a right to the reward.
  B. According to the above definition, there are no conditions in the covenant of grace.
    1. No man has a right to the reward.

2. The Covenant of Grace is a unilateral covenant.
3. Whatever can be conceived as a condition is all included in the universality of the promises.
4. The "conditions" are not so much conditions of the covenant as of the assurance that we shall continue in the covenant.

C. The role of faith in the Covenant of Grace.
1. Eternal life is promised to all those who believe even as it was promised to all those who obeyed in the Covenant of Works.
2. Faith is not a condition properly so-called.
3. Faith is the way, instrument or means by which we receive the promises of eternal life.
4. The difference between obedience in the Covenant of Works and faith in the Covenant of Grace is the difference between giving and receiving.

IV. The threatenings of the Covenant of Grace.
A. The Covenant of Grace has no threatenings peculiar to itself.
B. The threatenings are derived from the law from which every curse proceeds.

Chapter 2: Of the Oneness of the Covenant of Grace, as to its Substance.

I. The Oneness of the Covenant of Grace.
A. The Old and New Covenants are different with respect to "circumstantials."
B. The Old and New Covenants are the same with respect to their "substance."

II. The Oneness between the Old and New Testaments.
A. The one and same eternal life was promised to those in both covenants.
1. New Testament Evidence of the resurrection; John 5:39; Acts 24:14-15; Matt. 22:29.
2. Old Testament Evidence of the resurrection; Gen. 49:19; Job 19:25-27; Dan. 12:2.
B. Old Testament saints were saved by Christ; Acts 15:11; Heb. 13:8; 9:15; note also the necessary implication from John 14:6; Acts 4:12.
C. Old Testament saints were saved by faith; Hab. 2:4; Gen. 15:6; Ps. 2:12; Isa. 27:5; Heb. 11.

1. OT saints' faith was not a general faith but faith in Christ; John 8:56; Heb. 11:26; 1 Pet. 1:11.
2. Interpretation of Gal. 3:23:
    a. "Faith" here cannot mean that faith in Christ is new because Paul uses Abraham as an example for us; Gal. 3:6,7,9.
    b. Faith is meant as the faith of the redemption already completed as opposed to the hope of the OT saints.

Chapter 3: Of the Different Economies or Dispensations of the Covenant of Grace.

I. The difference between the two testaments.
  A. The difference consists in the administration of the testaments.
  B. The "circumstantial" differences of the testaments.
    1. In the Old Testament:
        a. The promised land as a pledge of heaven.
        b. Bondage to the elements of the world.
        c. The exclusion of the Gentiles.
        d. A less measure of the Spirit of grace.
    2. In the New Testament:
        a. The inheritance of the Gentiles.
        b. Freedom; liberty.
        c. A more plentiful measure of grace.

II. The different dispensations of the Old Testament.
  A. Adam to Noah.
  B. Noah to Abraham.
  C. Abraham to Moses.
  D. Moses to the New Covenant.

Chapter 4: Of Election.

I. Definition of Election: "Election is the eternal, free, and immutable counsel of God, about revealing the glory of his grace, in the eternal salvation of some certain persons."

II. Characteristics of election.
  A. Election is the counsel of God or decree; 2 Tim. 1:9; Eph. 1:11; Rom. 8:28; 9:11.
    1. It is important to distinguish between internal and external election, that is, the invisible and visible church.
    2. It is important to note the different uses of the "book of life."

B. Election is personal. It is not some general decree but a
   particular designation of certain individual persons to be saved.
   1. The term "predestinate" means to point out or ordain a
      certain person; Acts 17:31; 10:42; Rom. 1:4.
   2. Scriptural support: Luke 10:20; Phil. 4:3; 2 Tim. 2:19;
      John 13:18.
C. Election is eternal; Acts 11:18; Eph. 1:11,4; Rev. 13:8; 17:8;
   2 Tim. 1:9; 2 Thess. 2:13.
D. Election is unconditional.
   1. Scripture asserts that the most free will of God was the
      supreme reason or cause of election; Matt. 11:26; Luke 12:32;
      Rom. 9:21.
   2. Scripture asserts that foreseen good in man was not a
      reason for election; Rom. 9:11; 2 Tim. 1:9.
   3. Faith and holiness are gifts from God; Phil. 1:29; Eph. 2:8.
   4. The purpose or result of election is faith and holiness and
      thus cannot be the cause; Eph. 1:4; John 15:16; 2 Thess. 2:13.
E. Election is immutable.
   1. Immutability belongs to all the decrees of God in general;
      Isa. 14:27; 46:10; Rom. 9:19.
   2. God's decree is not suspended on a condition for if a
      condition is involved, the condition itself is at the same
      time decreed.
   3. The Scriptures ascribe immutability to the divine election;
      Rom. 9:11; 2 Tim. 2:19; Isa. 49:15-16; Rev. 3:5; Isa. 4:3.

III. The relation between election and assurance.
   A. Assurance is made possible because of God's election.
   B. How to attain the assurance of election.
      1. Need to apply the marks of election to yourself.
         a. Effectual calling by the word and Spirit of God; Rom. 8:30.
         b. Faith in God and Christ; 2 Thess. 2:13.
         c. Hatred and eschewing of evil; 2 Tim. 2:19.
         d. The sincere and constant study of holiness; Eph. 1:4;
            2 Thess. 2:13.
      2. The internal witness of the Spirit; Rom. 8:16; Eph. 1:13.
   C. Believers are to seek the assurance of their election.
      1. Cannot live a life of joy in the Lord without assurance.
      2. Cannot properly glorify God with a lack of valuing the
         grace and goodness of God.

3. Assurance promotes love for God by keeping his commandments.

Chapter 5: Of Effectual Calling.

I. Definition: "An act by which those, who are chosen by God, and redeemed by Christ, are sweetly invited, and effectually brought from a state of sin to a state of communion with God in Christ, both externally and internally."

II. The external call of God.
   A. The external call of God is proclaimed by natural revelation.
      1. The message of natural revelation; Psa. 19:1-4.
         a. To pursue heaven and eternity.
         b. To seek after God.
         c. That there is some hope of enjoying God due to the patience (2 Pet. 3:9) and goodness (Rom. 2:4) of God.
         d. Cannot enjoy God unless you pursue purity and holiness.
      2. The limits of natural revelation.
         a. Natural revelation renders men without excuse.
         b. Not sufficient for salvation.
   B. The external call of God is proclaimed by special revelation.
      1. Natural revelation provides the backdrop for special revelation.
      2. Special revelation is necessary for salvation; Rom. 10:14.
         a. Gospel call given in different ways and degrees over the course of history.
         b. Gospel call was never universal, as some have never heard it.
         c. The call contains the command to believe in Christ.
      3. The external call of special revelation must be accompanied by the internal call to be effectual.

III. The internal call of God.
   A. God exerts his infinite power, by which he converts the soul no less powerfully than sweetly.
   B. God's internal call does not interfere with the freedom of man.[3]
   C. Objections to the effectual call answered.

---

[3]Witsius writes, "God does not drag along the unwilling, by head and shoulders, but makes them willing, Phil. 2:13, bringing his truths so clearly to their understanding, that they cannot but assent, so effectually gaining upon their will by the charms of his goodness, that they are not able to reject them."

1. The complaints of God and Christ with respect to the unwillingness of the people refer to the external call.
2. With regard to the grieving of the Spirit we need to distinguish between the common operations of the Spirit and the moral and supernatural actions of the Spirit.

Chapter 6: Of Regeneration.

I. Definition: "Regeneration is that supernatural act of God, whereby a new and divine life is infused into the elect person spiritually dead, and that from the incorruptible seed of the word of God, made fruitful by the infinite power of the Spirit."

II. The meaning of spiritual death.
   A. Separated, alienated from God.
   B. Insensible of all spiritual things.
   C. Wholly incapable of any act of true life.

III. The different uses of the word "regeneration."
   A. The first act of passing from death to life.
      1. Regeneration in this sense is accomplished in a moment.
      2. There is no intermediate state between the regenerate and the unregenerate. For Scripture divides all of mankind into two classes, sheep and goats; Matt. 25:2-3.
   B. The second act or the manifestation of spiritual life.
      1. There are various degrees of regeneration in this sense of the term.
      2. Sometimes spiritual life manifests itself slowly as in regenerated infants.
      3. Hence, a person cannot always determine when he was saved.

IV. "Preparations" for regeneration.
   A. Semi-Pelagian view.
      1. The sinner prepares or comes to be regenerated by seeking, asking, repenting, sorrow for sin, etc.
      2. Witsius' response:
         a. A dead man or bad tree can do nothing to prepare himself for grace.
         b. Those who seem closest to heaven are furthest away; Matt. 19:21-22.
         c. Those who seem furthest away are saved; Matt. 21:31-32.

      d. God seeks them who seek Him not; Isa. 65:1.[4]
- B. A "Reformed" view.
    1. Preparations to regeneration.
        a. A breaking of the will.
        b. A serious consideration of the law.
        c. A consideration of their own sins and offences against God.
        d. A fear of hell and a despairing of their salvation.
    2. The differences between this view from the Semi-pelagian.
        a. These preparations are not from nature but the effects of the spirit of bondage preparing for actual regeneration.
        b. They do not merit regeneration.
    3. They are called preparations for grace and not effects or fruits of grace because the reprobate are able to perform these things.
    4. Witsius' response:
        a. These "preparations" of grace are not preparations but effects or fruits of regeneration.
        b. These "preparations" performed by the reprobate, no matter how they may appear, are still consistent with spiritual death and do not lead or prepare for conversion. A bad tree cannot bear good fruit.
- C. There are no "preparations" for regeneration in the sense of an act of passing from death to life.
- D. There are different degrees in regard to spiritual death.
    1. There are differences between infants and adults due to the fact that adults have had time to practice their evil habits.
    2. There are differences between adults due to God's restraining common grace.

V. The author of regeneration.
- A. God is the author of regeneration; John 1:13.
- B. Christ as God is the author of regeneration but also the meritorious and exemplary cause of our regeneration.
- C. The Holy Spirit is the author of regeneration; John 3:5.
    1. The water and the spirit of John 3:5 refer to the one and the same thing; namely the Holy Spirit and his regenerating work.

---

[4]Witsius writes, "We have not certainly received grace, because we are willing, but grace is given us while we are still unwilling."

    2. Scripture represents the Holy Spirit under the emblem of water; Isa. 44:3.

VI. The seed of regeneration.
- A. The seed of regeneration is the word of God.
- B. This seed does not always operate in the same manner as is clear in the case of infants.
- C. Hence, it is incumbent upon all men to place themselves under the teaching of the word of God.
- D. A person must encourage and nurture the beginning of grace in his life by engaging in the means of grace.

Chapter 7: Of Faith.
- I. The acts of faith.
  - A. Knowledge of the thing to be believed.
    - 1. Arguments for the knowledge aspect of faith.
      - a. Scripture testifies that faith involves knowledge; Isa. 53:11; John 17:3 cp. Heb. 2:4; John 6:69; 2 Tim. 1:3.
      - b. The nature of faith dictates knowledge. Assent to something presupposes knowledge.
      - c. Faith is produced externally from the preaching of the word and internally by the teaching of the Holy Spirit.
    - 2. The amount of knowledge will vary from believer to believer.
    - 3. The increase of knowledge strengthens faith.
    - 4. The things that must be believed in order to be saved.
      - a. The divinity of the Scriptures.
      - b. Certain truths with respect to salvation in Christ.
        - i. Knowledge of your sin.
        - ii. Christ is the only Saviour.
        - iii. Salvation is obtained through faith.
  - B. Assent to and conviction of the truths of the gospel; Heb. 11:1.
    - 1. Conviction is based upon the truth of God.
    - 2. If faith is assent, can true faith ever waver?
      - a. Perfect faith never wavers, which is what we are to strive after.
      - b. The best of believers will waver due to defects of faith arising from sin.
      - c. Faith will continually wrestle with temptations until heaven.

C. Love of the truth; 2 Thess. 2:10.
D. A hunger and thirst after Christ.
E. A receiving of Christ the Lord for salvation; John 1:12; Col. 2:6.
F. Reclining and staying upon Christ; Isa. 48:2.
G. Must receive Christ *as* Lord; Col. 2:6.[5]
H. Applying the promises of the gospel to oneself or making the promises personal; Gal. 2:20.

II. Non-saving faith.
   A. Historical faith is theoretical or naked assent.
   B. Temporary faith engages the heart but only for a time.
   C. Distinctions between non-saving and saving faith.
      1. Non-saving faith does not properly see the beauty of or love the truth.
      2. Non-saving faith does not engage in self-examination.
      3. The joy of non-saving faith arises from novelty and rarity of the truth, which does not produce the love of God.
      4. Non-saving faith does not produce proper fruit.

III. The assurance of one's faith.
   A. Assurance of faith is possible; 2 Tim. 1:12; 2 Cor. 13:5.
   B. Examine oneself according to the acts of faith.
   C. Causes of doubt in believers.
      1. A wrong notion of saving faith.
      2. Unable to properly discern the proper acts of one's own heart.
      3. Comparing one's faith with the level of faith that is aspired.
   D. Reasons for gaining the assurance of your faith.
      1. Assurance produces gratefulness to God.
      2. Consolation for ourselves.
      3. Assurance produces piety and obedience.

Chapter 8: Of Justification.
I. The meaning of the term "justify."
   A. Normally used in a declarative sense: to account, declare, prove; Psa. 82:3; Deut. 25:1; Prov. 17:15; Isa. 5:22-23; Psa. 51:4; Matt. 11:19; Luke 7:29.

---

[5]Witsius writes, "When the believer so receives Christ and leans upon him, he not only considers him as a Saviour but also as a Lord. For he receives a whole Christ, and receiveth him just as he is: but he is no less Lord than a Saviour. Yea, he cannot be a Saviour unless he be likewise a Lord."

    1. Both Roman Catholics and Protestants alike agree that "justify" is not always used in a forensic sense.

    2. Witsius only finds two places where "justify" means more than a mere declaration of righteousness; Isa. 53:11; Dan. 12:3.

  B. It is used with reference to particular actions of men.

    1. In an absolute sense; Psa. 106:30-31.

    2. In a comparative sense; Jer. 3:11; Ez. 16:31.

  C. It is used with reference to the state of man.

II. Definition: "It is a judicial, but gracious act of God, whereby the elect and believing sinner, is absolved from the guilt of his sins, and hath a right to eternal life adjudged to him, on account of the obedience of Christ, received by faith."

III. The Judge who declares a sinner righteous.

  A. God the Father; Rom. 8:33; Isa. 43:25; Jam. 4:12; Rom. 3:6.

  B. God the Son; John 5:22,27; Matt. 9:2.

  C. God the Spirit in the sense of applying and sealing it to believers; 1 Cor. 2:12; Rom. 8:16.

IV. The matter (ground) of justification.

  A. It is the perfect righteousness of Christ alone; 2 Cor. 5:21.

  B. There is nothing that we add to the righteousness of Christ; Gal. 2:21.

V. The form of justification consists in two acts.

  A. The discharging of unrighteousness.

    1. Removes the power of condemnation.

    2. Removes the dominion of sin.

  B. The adjudging of righteousness.

    1. Forgiveness of sins.

    2. Right to eternal life.

VI. The instrument by which we receive the righteousness of Christ and justification.

  A. We are justified by faith alone; Gal. 2:16; Rom. 3:28.

  B. The sense in which we are justified by faith.

    1. Not in the sense that faith replaces obedience.

    2. Faith is not strictly a condition of justification.

      a. Reformed creeds say otherwise.

      b. Faith is not a work that merits justification.

       c. The condition of justification is perfect obedience.

       d. Need to distinguish between faith and the works of faith.

    3. "The genuine opinion of the reformed is this: that faith justifies, as it is the bond of our strictest union with Christ, by which all things that are Christ's become also ours or… as it is the acceptance of the gift offered, rendering the donation firm and irrevocable."

VII. The article(s) or time period(s) of our justification.
   A. General time of justification.
     1. Immediately after the fall.
     2. At Christ's death.
   B. Particular time of justification.
     1. At the time of conversion.
     2. God's declaration in heaven.
     3. Admittance into friendship with God.
     4. After death.
     5. At the day of judgment.
       a. Declaration of being righteous and holy based upon inherent righteousness.
       b. Declaration of right to eternal life based upon the righteousness of Christ.

VIII. The uses of the doctrine of justification.
   A. Displays the glory, goodness, justice and wisdom of God.
   B. Removes all boasting in the sinner; Isa. 64:6; 1 Cor. 4:7.
   C. Comforts those who realize that there is nothing in themselves that would merit God's favor.
   D. Promotes godliness.
     1. Humility,
     2. Obedience.
     3. Love.

Chapter 9: Of Spiritual Peace.

I. Definition: "A mutual concord between God and the sinner, who is justified by faith; so that the heart of God is carried out towards man, and in like manner, the heart of man towards God, by a delightful inclination of friendship."

II. The origin of spiritual peace.
   A. Spiritual peace presupposes war.

   B. God is the one who originates peace with man.
     1. Due to God's mercy and love.
     2. God seeks man; freely offers peace to all men.
     3. God subdues His elect.

III. The consequences of spiritual peace.
   A. Friendship with God.
   B. Peace of conscience; Rom. 14:7; Eph. 3:12.
   C. Peace with fellow believers and angels.
   D. Peace with the whole of creation; Isa. 14:11-12; Hos. 2:18.

IV. Man's role with regard to spiritual peace.
   A. Man's responsibility in seeking spiritual peace.
     1. Confess his sins before God.
     2. Believe in Christ alone for reconciliation with God.
     3. Humbly submit himself to God.
   B. Man's responsibility in preserving spiritual peace.
     1. Daily love for God; John 14:21.
     2. Frequent communion with God.
     3. Walk in obedience to God; John 14:23.
     4. Return to God when you fall into sin; Jer. 3:22.
     5. Submit to God's providence in your life.

V. The interruption of spiritual peace.
   A. Believers can never completely lose peace with God.
   B. The sense of peace with God can be interrupted.
     1. God does not always draw near; Isa. 8:17; Ps. 10:1.
     2. God at times is displeased with his children; Ps. 80:4.
     3. God at times is angry with his children; Ps. 88:16-18; Isa. 57:17.
     4. Sometimes God deals with us as an adversary; Job 13:24-27.
     5. Gives us over to be vexed and buffeted by the devil; Job 2:6.
   C. Reasons for the interruption of spiritual peace.
     1. Reasons from God's perspective.
       a. To demonstrate the sovereignty of God; Matt. 10:15.
       b. To show the difference between this life and the one to come.
       c. To demonstrate the excellence of his grace.
       d. To demonstrate the power and goodness of God in preserving the soul through many trials and sorrows.
     2. Reasons from man's perspective.

a. Reasons in regard to the past.
   i. Guilty of a grievous sin; Isa. 63:10.
   ii. Lack of fearing God.
   iii. Carnal security and pride.
   iv. Unworthy acceptance of divine grace.
b. Reasons in regard to the future.
   i. That God may try and test our faith; 1 Pet. 1:6-7.
   ii. To cause us to pray.
   iii. To make us wise.
   iv. To heighten our appreciation and preservation of God's grace.
D. What one can do to retrieve the sense of peace with God.
  1. Discover the reason or cause; Lam. 3:40.
  2. Renew your faith and repentance.
  3. Be much in prayer for help.
  4. Wait patiently upon God to restore you; Lam. 3:26.

Chapter 10: Of Adoption.

I. The sons of God.
  A. All believers are sons of God; 1 John 3:1-2.
  B. Adam was a son of God; Luke 3:38.

II. The ways in which the elect become children of God.
  A. Born of God; John 1:12-13.
  B. Marriage with the Lord Jesus.
  C. Adoption.

III. The relationship between the Old and New Testament.
  A. Old Testament believers were adopted as sons though placed under tutelage.
    1. Not admitted into the mysteries of God's will.
    2. Unable to approach the holy of holies.
    3. Their inheritance was the land of Canaan.
  B. New Testament believers are not subject to OT tutelage.
    1. Introduced into the Father's secret counsels.
    2. Free access to the Father.
    3. Not subject to a typical inheritance.

IV. The blessings bequeathed to the sons of God.
  A. Extraordinary blessings; 1 Cor. 2:9.
  B. The glory of our elder brother.

C. Great and precious promises; 2 Pet. 1:4.
  1. The whole world; both present and future.
  2. A spiritual kingdom.
     a. The dignity of being a son of God.
     b. Victory over sin; Rom. 6:14,18.
     c. Crushing of Satan; Rom. 16:20.
     d. Triumph over a whole conquered world.
     e. Inestimable riches of spiritual gifts.
     f. Peace of soul and joy in the Holy Spirit; Rom. 14:17.
  3. God Himself.
     a. Protection from every evil.
     b. Communication of every good.

Chapter 11: Of The Spirit of Adoption.
I. Definition: "The spirit of adoption is the Holy Spirit, operating those things in the elect, which are suitable to, and becoming the sons of God, who love God, and are beloved by him."

II. The role of the Spirit in the Old Testament.
  A. The Holy Spirit was bestowed upon OT believers; Num. 14:24; Neh. 9:20; Ps. 143:10; 51:10-12; Isa. 63:8,11.
  B. The work of the Spirit that is common in both testament periods.
    1. A persuasion of the greatest love of the adopter; Psa. 4:7; 31:7; 51:14; 36:7-9; 63:5.
    2. Obedience due to filial love; Ps. 81:1; 116:1; 119:10.
    3. An expectation of the inheritance; Psa. 17:25; 31:19.
  C. The work of the Spirit in the OT was more rare and sparing and mixed with much terror.
    1. The covenant of grace was revealed more obscurely.
    2. Therefore, the operations of the Spirit were obscure; so obscure, comparatively speaking that the Spirit is said not to have been under the Old; John 7:39.
  D. The Holy Spirit is promised in the OT; Isa. 35:6-7; 44:3; Ez. 34:26-27; Joel 2:28; Zech. 14:8.

III. The work of the Spirit of adoption.
  A. Enables believers to cry "Abba, Father"; Rom. 8:15-16.
  B. Together with our spirit bears witness that we are children of God; Rom. 8:15-16.
  C. The testimony of our conscience must be well grounded.

    1. Based upon the marks of a child of God.
       a. Imitation of our Father.
       b. A new life that is worthy of God and his grace.
       c. A true and sincere love for God.
       d. A filial fear and obedience; Mal. 1:6; 1 Pet. 1:17.
       e. Unfeigned brotherly love.
    2. Examine ourselves according to those marks.

Chapter 12: Of Sanctification.

I. The meaning of "holy."
    A. That which is separated from a promiscuous and civil, but especially from a profane use; Lev. 20:26; 2 Cor. 6:17.
    B. Whatever is dedicated to, or set apart for God and his service; Ex. 30:29; 19:5; 1 Chron. 23:13.
    C. Purity.

II. Definition: "Sanctification is that real work of God, by which they, who are chosen, regenerated, and justified, are continually more and more transformed from the turpitude of sin, to the purity of the divine image."

III. The meaning of sanctification.
    A. The difference between sanctification and effectual calling.
       1. The effect of effectual calling is union with Christ.
       2. The effect of sanctification is the exercise of holy habits and graces.
    B. The difference between sanctification and justification.
       1. "Justification is a judicial act, terminating in a relative change of state; namely, a freedom from punishment and a right to life."
       2. "Sanctification is a work...which terminates in a change of state as to the quality both of habits and actions."
    C. The different uses of the term sanctification.
       1. Broadly speaking, it refers to the whole of man's salvation.
       2. Narrowly speaking, it refers to the above definition.

IV. The process or work of sanctification.
    A. The first step is to put off or mortify the old man; Col. 2:9; Eph. 4:22.
       1. The whole of man has been corrupted with sin and so needs to be put off.

a. The understanding; Eph. 4:18; 1 Cor. 2:14.
b. The will; Job 21:14; Hos. 8:12; Micah 3:2.
c. The affections; Rom. 1:26.
d. The body; Ps. 119:37; Prov. 23:2.
2. Putting off or mortification is the destruction of the dominion of sin and the purging of corruptions.
B. The second step is to put on or vivification of the new man; Col. 3:10; Eph. 4:24.
1. The whole of man needs to be changed or sanctified.
2. Sanctification does not consist only in the amendment of our actions but in the conferring of new habits (due to the utter corruption of our nature); 2 Pet. 1; Heb. 5:14; 1 Cor. 13:13.
3. The relation between the different faculties of man.
a. The understanding is illuminated by the Holy Spirit to the truth of God.
b. The understanding of the truth affects the will.
c. The understanding and will thus affect the feelings.
d. The actions of the body are determined by the above.
e. The righteous understanding and will must rule over the feelings when they are sinful; 1 Cor. 9:27.

V. The author and efficient cause of sanctification.
A. God is the author of our sanctification; 1 Thess. 5:23.
B. The Holy Spirit; 2 Thess. 2:13; Tit. 2:5.
C. Christ as to merit and application; Eph. 5:26.

VI. The three aspects of the Christian life.
A. The original and/or motives for growing in holiness.
1. Grace; 1 Cor. 15:10.
2. Faith; Heb. 11:6.
a. Faith purifies the heart; Acts 15:9.
b. Faith restores us to God.
c. Knowing Christ is necessary to love God.
d. Faith unites us to the living Christ.
3. Love.
a. Love for God.
b. Love for ourselves; Eph. 5:29; Heb. 11:6.
c. Love for our neighbor.
B. The rule or standard for holiness.
1. The standards for the heathen are the nature of man; right reason; the examples of excellent men.

 2. The Christian standard.
  a. The written law of God.
  b. The examples of the saints and especially Christ who is the perfect example.
 C. The goal or end of holiness.
  1. The glory of God; 1 Cor. 10:31.
  2. One's own end or happiness.
   a. Assurance of salvation.
   b. To rejoice in a clean conscience.
   c. To enjoy the love of God in Christ.
   d. To live at ease in the salvation of God.
   e. Our end is not the ultimate but is to be directed to the glory of God.[6]
  3. Our neighbor's end or happiness; Matt. 5:16.

VII. The means of sanctification.
 A. The word of God and devout meditation of it; John 17:17.
  1. Must be diligently, daily read.
  2. Must be heard in preaching; Rom. 10:14,15,17.
  3. It must be kept and valued.
  4. One must meditate upon it.
  5. Must be at hand to use in times of temptation.
 B. The attentive consideration of the Lord Jesus.
 C. The practice of devout prayer; 1 John 5:14.
 D. Submission to the government and guidance of the Holy Spirit.
 E. Renew our covenant with God.
 F. Examination of conscience.
 G. Willingly and thankfully heeding rebuke; Prov. 15:12; Ps. 141:5.

VIII. The doctrine of Perfectionism.
 A. We cannot attain unto perfection in this life.
  1. Testimony of Scripture; 1 Kings 8:46; Eccl. 7:28; Prov. 20:9; Jam. 3:2; 1 John 1:8.
  2. The confession of saints; Ps. 19:12; Rom. 7:18-19; Phil. 3:13-14; Isa. 64:6.
  3. Examples of the saints.

---

[6]Witsius writes, "And thus it is, that, while they piously aim at the happiness promised to them, and seek their own glory in the proper order and measure, they, at the same time, 'rejoice in the hope of the glory of God,' Rom. 5:2. For then they are made happy, 'when God is glorified and admired in them,' 2 Thess. 1:10."

B. The cause of imperfection is our indwelling flesh or corruption; Gal. 5:17; Rom. 7:15-16.[7]
   1. "Flesh" refers to remaining corruption, which abides in the whole man (body and soul) but its principal seat is in the soul itself.
   2. The war within is not between body and soul but between sanctifying grace and the remains of natural corruption.
C. Reasons God does not grant perfection to us in this life.
   1. To display the difference between heaven and earth.
   2. To teach us patience, humility, and sympathy.
   3. To teach that salvation is by grace alone.
   4. To demonstrate the wisdom of God.
D. The biblical usage of the term "perfect."
   1. A perfection of sincerity or integrity; Job 1:1.
   2. A perfection of parts.
      a. Subjectively with regard to the whole man.
      b. Objectively with respect to the law.
   3. A comparative perfection; 1 Cor. 2:6.
   4. An evangelical perfection: perfection in Christ.
   5. A perfection in degrees which we will not achieve until glory.

Chapter 13: Of Conservation.
I. Definition: "Conservation is a gracious work of God, whereby he so keeps the elect, the redeemed, the regenerated, the faithful and the sanctified, though in themselves weak, and apt to fall away, internally by the most powerful efficacy of his Spirit, externally by the means which he has wisely appointed for that purpose, that they shall never quite lose the habits of those graces once infused into them, but be certainly brought, by a steadfast perseverance, to eternal salvation."

II. The role of the Trinity in conservation.
A. God the Father.
   1. Predestined the elect to eternal salvation.
   2. Gave believers to Christ for his inheritance; Ps. 2:8; John 17:6; 10:29.
   3. Promised to not allow the elect to fall from grace to their eternal destruction; Isa. 54:10; Jer. 32:38-40; 31:31-33.

---

[7]Witsius quotes Bernard on indwelling flesh: "It dwells, but reigns not, abides, but neither rules nor prevails; in some measure it is rooted out, but not quite expelled: cast down, but not entirely cast out."

4. God keeps his elect by his almighty power; 1 Pet. 1:5.
B. God the Son.
   1. Jesus keeps those whom he bought with his blood; John 17:12.
   2. Jesus prays that the elect be kept safe; John 17:15,20.
   3. Jesus builds his house with real stones (1 Pet. 2:5) which does not crumble.
   4. Jesus unites the elect (corporately and individually) to himself and thus they are safe; Eph. 5:23.
C. God the Holy Spirit.
   1. Continually abides in believers; John 14:16-17.
   2. Is the spring of eternal life in the elect.
   3. Author of our seal confirming our salvation; Eph. 1:13; 2 Cor. 1:21-22; 2 Tim. 2:19.
   4. Gives to us a down payment of our eternal salvation; Eph. 1:14.

III. The method or means God uses to preserve us.
A. His infinite and supernatural power.
B. His word containing promises, threatenings, exhortations, and admonitions to excite us to persevere in the faith.

IV. The doctrine of conservation promotes piety and upholds truth.
A. This doctrine promotes the power, goodness, holiness, and the efficacy of the merits and intercession of Christ; and the power of the Holy Spirit.
B. This doctrine allures the unconverted for the promise of eternal life is more sure and stable. The opposite doctrine promotes procrastinating repentance until the end of one's life.
C. This doctrine motivates one to grow in holiness.[8]

Chapter 14: Of Glorification.
I. Definition: "Glorification is the gracious act of God, whereby he actually translates his chosen and redeemed people, from an unhappy and base, to a happy and glorious state."

II. The time of glorification.
A. Glorification is begun in this life with the first fruits.
B. Glorification is consummated in the life to come.
   1. The intermediate state.
   2. The eternal state.

---

[8]Witsius writes, "Nothing is more powerful for inflaming our hearts with love to God, than the knowledge, sense, and taste of the divine love shed abroad in them."

III. The first fruits of glorification.
    A. Holiness.
    B. The vision of God which is apprehended by:
        1. Faith; 2 Cor. 5:7; Heb. 11:1.
        2. Experimental sense of his goodness; Ps. 34:8.
        3. The imagination of sick and dying Christians.
    C. The gracious possession and enjoyment of God; Ps. 145:15.
    D. Full assurance of the eternal state to come.
    E. Joy unspeakable; 1 Pet. 1:8.

IV. The intermediate state.
    A. The human soul survives death; Matt. 22:32 (cf. Luke 20:38);
        Phil. 1:23; Heb. 12:23; Luke 16; Psa. 31:5; Acts 7:59; Luke 23:43.
    B. The human soul lives, understands and feels either the favour
        or vengeance of God after death; Luke 20:38; Elijah; Matt. 17:3;
        Phil. 1:23; 2 Cor. 5:8; Rev. 14:15; 1 Cor. 15:19, 30-32.
    C. Souls of believers are received into heavenly joys and mansions;
        ·2 Cor. 5:1; Luke 23:43.
        1. Joy of being with God and Christ in glory; John 12:26; 17:24.
        2. Joy of seeing God in the light of glory; Matt. 5:8.
        3. Joy of loving God.
        4. Joy of dwelling in holiness and glory.
        5. Joy more than inexpressible, more than glorious.

V. The blessedness of the eternal state for believers.
    A. The resurrection of the body; 1 Cor. 15.
        1. The body will be the same for such is implied in the term
            "resurrection."
        2. The quality of the body will be changed.
            a. All infirmities will be removed.
            b. A spiritual or heavenly body that will be able to
               inherit the kingdom of God (1 Cor. 15:50); that is a
               body that does not require meat and drink.
    B. A greater glory in the perfections God has manifested in His works.
        1. The redemption of all creation; Rom. 8:19-20.
        2. The divine judgment.
        3. The gathering together of the elect as one perfect body.
        4. Conforming us to the image of Christ.
    C. The redemptive work of God shall be complete which will be
        immutable and eternal; Matt. 25:46; Rom. 2:7; 1 Pet. 5:4;
        1 Thess. 4:17.

VI. There will be a difference in quality and quantity of rewards among the elect; Rom. 2:6; 2 Cor. 5:10; 9:6; Gal. 6:8; 1 Cor. 3:8; Matt. 19:28.

Book 4

Chapter 1: Of the Doctrine of Salvation in the first age of the World.
I. The first proclamation of the gospel; Gen. 3:14-15.
   A. The devil and not the serpent is condemned; cf. 2 Cor. 11:3; Rev. 12:9; Rom. 16:20.
   B. The blessings or benefits promised to man.
     1. The curse of the serpent.
     2. The destruction of the devil's power.
     3. The enmity placed between the serpent and the woman and her seed; which includes man's sanctification.
     4. The resurrection of the body.
   C. Jehovah God is the author of these benefits.
   D. The meritorious cause of these benefits is the seed of the woman.
     1. Seed is used collectively but also in an eminent sense it refers to Jesus Christ.
     2. Christ is therefore the meritorious cause of these benefits.
   E. The manner of acquisition of these benefits are the sufferings of the Seed as indicated by "thou shalt bruise his heel."
   F. The heirs of the benefits.
     1. Adam and Eve.
     2. The seed of the woman, i.e., the godly seed of the woman; Rom. 9:8.
   G. The instrument by which the heirs partake of the benefits is faith as is indicated by:
     1. The use of the common term "seed" which signifies our union with Christ which is by faith.
     2. The conquering of the devil which is performed by Christ as well as by the elect in Christ by faith.

II. The faith of Adam and Eve.
   A. Adam's faith is demonstrated by calling his wife Eve.
   B. Eve's faith is demonstrated by her words of hope in the promise when Cain and Seth were born.

III. The term "sons of God" refers to the godly and the "sons of man" refer to the ungodly.

Chapter 2: Of The Doctrine of Grace under Noah.

I. The doctrine of grace in the naming of Noah.
  A. The righteous must contend with sin.
  B. There is good and comfort to be expected.
  C. God is the author of the good.

II. The doctrine of grace in the preaching of Noah.
  A. Noah was a preacher of righteousness; 2 Pet. 2:5.
  B. Noah preached the doctrine of salvation by the the Spirit of Christ; 1 Pet. 3:19-20.

III. The doctrine of grace in the blessing with which Noah blesses his sons; Gen. 9:26-27.
  A. God is the author of blessing.
  B. Shem and his posterity are to be God's peculiar people.
  C. The doctrine of election for the younger is preferred over the older.
  D. The sins of the fathers are visited upon their children as in the case of Canaan.
  E. Godliness profits soul and body as material blessings are promised to Japheth.
  F. Word of grace has a great power of alluring and persuading.
  G. Church on earth is to resemble tabernacles as they are to expect permanent habitation in heaven.
  H. Divine majesty was to rise from the posterity of Shem and dwell in his tents.
  I. The Gentiles, especially the descendants of Japheth, were to be allured by the preaching of the gospel to the communion of the church of Israel.

Chapter 3: Of the Doctrine of Grace from Abraham to Moses.

I. The doctrine of grace under Abraham.
  A. Grace seen in the appearances of God to Abraham.
    1. God's calling him out of Ur; Gen. 12:1.
    2. Near Shechem; Gen. 12:67.
    3. In Bethel; Gen. 13:3-4.
    4. Promised a son and heir; Gen. 15.
    5. Circumcision; Gen. 17:1.
    6. When God became his guest; Gen. 18:1.
    7. God approved of Sarah's proposal to cast out Hagar and Ishmael; Gen. 21:12.

        8. Commanded him to offer up Isaac in sacrifice; Gen. 22:1.
- B. Grace seen in the covenant God made with Abraham.
    1. Time frame of the Covenant: 430 years before the Exodus; Gal. 3:17.
        a. 215 years from Abraham's entering into Canaan to Jacob's entering Egypt.
        b. 215 years of dwelling and bondage of the Israelites in Egypt.
    2. The stipulations of the covenant.
        a. The leaving of his country which involved self-denial; Gen. 12:1.
        b. Of not fearing which involved faith and love; Gen. 15:1.
        c. Of walking before God which involved holiness; Gen. 17:1.
    3. The promises of the covenant.
        a. The spiritual promises of the covenant.
            i. General spiritual promises; Gen. 15:1; 17:1,7.
                aa. Protection against every evil.
                bb. God Himself as reward.
                cc. Communion and fruition of God.
                dd. Continuance of the favor of God.
            ii. The special spiritual promises to Abraham.
                aa. He is the head and honorary father of all believers, for the Messiah would be his descendent, and he is the pattern of faith and blessing to those after him; Gen. 12:2-3.
                bb. He is promised a seed which refers to:
                    (1). Isaac; Gen. 21:12.
                    (2). Christ; Gal. 3:16.
                    (3). All Believers; Rom. 9:8.
        b. The corporal or external promises to Abraham.
            i. The multiplication of his seed by Isaac; Gen. 13:16; 15:5; 17:2; 22:16.
            ii. The inheritance of the land of Canaan; Gen. 12:7; 13:15; 15:17; 17:7.
            iii. The deliverance from the Egyptian bondage; Gen. 15:13-14.
- C. The faith of Abraham.
    1. Abraham was justified by faith alone; Gen. 15:6; Rom. 4:3; Gal. 3:6.
    2. The object of his faith.

a. Generally it was in all the promises made to him; Rom. 4:20-21.

b. His faith was in Christ; John 8:56.

II. The doctrine of grace under Isaac and Jacob.

A. The promises made to Abraham were confirmed to Isaac; Gen. 26:4.

B. The doctrine of election was taught in the oracle concerning Jacob and Esau; Gen. 25:23.

C. The promises made to Abraham and Isaac were confirmed to Jacob; Gen. 28:13-15.

D. Jacob declared the promises applied to his twelve sons and specifically exalted Judah from whom the Messiah would be descended; Gen. 49:10.

E. Christ is spoken of in the blessing imparted to the tribe of Naphthali; Gen. 49:21.

III. The doctrine of grace elsewhere until Moses.

A. Job's proclamation of faith in God; Job 7:20. Here Job called God the Notzer (keeper or preserver) of men.

B. Elihu spoke of the Messiah; Job 33:23-24. Here he spoke of:

1. The excellence of the Messiah.

2. His offices.

3. His benefits.

C. Balaam spoke of the Messiah; Num. 24:15-19.

1. This prophecy in a diminutive sense refers to David.

2. In a higher sense it refers to Christ.

Chapter 4: Of the Decalogue.

I. The promulgation of the the Ten Commandments.

A. God is the law-giver or legislator.

1. The Trinity is to be acknowledged as law-giver.

2. Nonetheless the Son of God in a peculiar respect is to be considered the law-giver.

B. The attending ministers at the giving of the law.

1. Angels were present as ministers; Acts 7:53.

a. Their presence added to the majestic pomp of the Law-giver; Deut. 33:2.

b. The words of God were formed in the air by angels.

c. The tablets were delivered to Moses by angels; Gal. 3:19.

      2. Moses was a minister of God; Deut. 33:4; 5:4-6; Lev. 26:46; Mal. 4:4; John 1:17.
- C. The time is fifty days after the Exodus; Ex. 19:1.
- D. The place was Mount Sinai; Deut. 5:2; Ex. 3:1.
  1. The barrenness of the land signified that the law by itself cannot redeem fallen man.
  2. The proclamation from the mountain in the hearing of all signified the universality of the moral law.
- E. The manner of the giving of the law.
  1. Accompanied with awesome signs of thunder, lightning, smoke, earthquakes; Ex. 19:16,18; Deut. 4:11; Heb. 12:18.
     a. To proclaim the majesty of the Law-giver and instill the fear of God in the people so that they might obey; Ex. 20:20.
     b. To display the nature of the law.
     c. To test the faith of the people; Ex. 20:20.
  2. No visible form of God was seen; Deut. 4:12,15.
- F. The publishing of the law.
  1. Law consisted of ten words; Ex. 34:18; Deut. 4:13.
     a. Prescription of duties.
     b. Threatenings for disobedience derived from covenant of works.
     c. Promises for obedience derived from covenant of grace.
  2. Law was written by the finger of God; Ex. 24:12; 31:18; Deut. 9:10.
     a. So the law would remain throughout the ages, hence tablets are called "the tables of testimony"; Ex. 31:18; 34:29.
     b. To demonstrate the pre-eminence of this law over human laws and other divine laws written by Moses.
     c. To intimate that it is the work of God alone, to write the law on the heart.
  3. Law written on two tables of stone.
     a. Both sides of the tables were written upon; Ex. 32:15.
     b. Cannot determine the number of precepts inscribed on each table.
  4. The tables were placed in the ark under the mercy seat; Ex. 25:16; Deut. 5:5; 1 Kings 8:9.

II. The binding nature of the decalogue.
- A. The decalogue is the same as the law of nature therefore it is always binding.

B. God's authorship requires us to obey.

C. The Gentiles were not bound to the decalogue only in so far as it was published or given to Israel; Rom. 2:12.

D. God's commandment to one applies to all.

E. God did add special motives for obedience for Israel though this does not abrogate the law for Gentiles.

F. There is only one church, one kingdom, one king, and one law which remains binding to all; Eph. 2:14; Rom. 11:17.

G. The manner in which the law was proclaimed and published implies its universality.

H. The New Testament confirms the binding nature of the law; Matt. 5:17; Rom. 13:9; James 2:8-11; Eph. 6:2.

I. Only God can abrogate his law and he has not done so.

J. The law as a covenant of works is abrogated.

III. The use of the law.

A. The use of the law in itself or absolutely.

   1. A representation of virtue, goodness, and holiness.

   2. The way in which man can have glorious communion with God; Lev. 18:5; Rom. 7:10.

   3. A command of God binding everyone upon the pain of death.

B. The use of the law relative to the state of man.

   1. Pre-fallen state of man.

     a. Rule of obedience.

     b. Beautiful ornament of man.

     c. Condition of covenant of works.

   2. Fallen state of man.

     a. Discover and convince man of his sin; Rom. 3:20.

       i. Law acts as a mirror; James 1:23.

       ii. Law entices man to sin; Rom. 7:7,13.

     b. To denounce the curse against man; Rom. 3:19.

     c. To restrain man; 1 Tim. 1:9.

     d. To bring sinners to Christ; Rom. 10:4; Gal. 3:24.

       i. Restrains unregenerate from falling too far.

       ii. Strips man of self-righteousness and self-hope.

   3. State of restoration.

     a. To show us what Christ had to do on our behalf.

     b. To show us how far we have to go to be perfect.

     c. Rule of obedience.

      d. Bears witness, approves, and commends the sanctification and thus the assurance of the elect.

IV. The decalogue as a covenant.
- A. The decalogue is called a covenant; Ex. 34:28; Deut. 5:2; 4:13; 9:9.
- B. The covenant contained stipulations (Ex. 19:5-6), and promises (Ex. 20:12).
- C. The relation of this covenant to the covenant of works and grace.
  1. There was a repetition of the doctrine concerning the law of the covenant of works; Lev. 18:5.
  2. There was a repetition of the covenant of works.
  3. The repetition of the covenant of works did not include the establishment of the covenant of works; Gal. 3:17.
     - a. Covenant of works was abrogated.
     - b. Purpose of repetition was to convict of sin and drive the people to Christ.
  4. There was repetition of some of the things belonging to the covenant of grace.
  5. The Mosaic covenant was not formally the covenant of works.
     - a. Covenant of works cannot be established with a sinner.
     - b. God did not require perfect obedience as a condition of the covenant or as a cause of receiving the reward.
     - c. The curse of the covenant of works was not included.
     - d. Gal. 4:24-25: Paul does not consider the Mosaic covenant as it was intended by God but how the Jews had perverted it into a covenant of works.
  6. The Mosaic covenant was not formally a covenant of grace.
     - a. Covenant of grace requires not only obedience but also promises and strength to obey.
     - b. These things do not appear at Sinai as is seen in the difference between the Mosaic and New covenants; Jer. 31:31-34.
     - c. This does not mean that the godly did not have the strength to obey but only that this strength did not come from the Mosaic covenant but the covenant of grace, which was also theirs.
- D. The Mosaic covenant was a national covenant.
  1. "A national covenant between God and Israel, whereby Israel promised to God a sincere obedience to all his precepts, especially to the ten words; God, on the other hand, promised to Israel, that such an observance would

be acceptable to him, nor want its reward, both in this life, and in that which is to come, both as to soul and body."

   2. "This [covenant] is a consequent both of the covenant of grace and of works; but was formally neither the one nor the other."

E. The decalogue is not the form of a covenant properly so called but the rule of duty.

Chapter 5: Of the Doctrine of the Prophets.

I. The Old Testament prophets clearly spoke of the person and work of Christ; 1 Pet. 1:10-11; Acts 10:43; 26:22-23.

II. Witsius does not elaborate further on this subject. He writes, "this subject has been, both formerly and lately, considered by the learned, and treated with such accuracy, that I have nothing to add."

Chapter 6: Of the Types.

I. The interpretation of the types of the Old Testament.

  A. There are two senses to most things in the Old Testament.

    1. The literal sense or meaning.

    2. The mystical sense or meaning which points to Christ, in his person, states, offices, and works and in his spiritual body, the church.

  B. We have a duty to interpret the types of the Old Testament.

    1. An infallible authority is not necessary for interpretation even as it is not necessary to interpret other parts of Scripture.

    2. Not all types are explained in the New Testament even as not all prophecies are explained in the New Testament.

  C. Guidelines of interpretation.

    1. The doctrine of Christ is the key of knowledge without which nothing can be savingly understood in Moses and prophets; Lk. 11:42.

    2. Use the NT to interpret the OT.

    3. Proceed with fear and trembling lest you misinterpret.

    4. Not every circumstance of a type of Christ has significance.

    5. Some types there is only a faint resemblance to Christ.

    6. Some types refer to both Christ and the church.

  D. The three kinds or classes of types.

      1. Natural types.
      2. Historical types.
      3. Legal types.

II. The natural types of the Old Testament.
    A. The creation of the world.
    B. The creation of man and woman.

III. The historical types of the Old Testament.
    A. The first age of the world.
      1. Abel represented Christ in his humiliation.
      2. Enoch represented Christ in his exaltation.
    B. The second period.
      1. Noah with respect to:
        a. Himself which represented Christ.
        b. The ark which represented Christ and the church.
        c. The deluge which represented Christ and the church.
      2. Isaac with respect to:
        a. His person which represents Christ.
        b. His offering which represents Christ.
        c. His deliverance which represents the church.
    C. The Mosaic period.
      1. Moses represented Christ as:
        a. Deliverer.
        b. Mediator.
        c. Prophet.
      2. Aaron represented Christ as high priest.

IV. The legal types of the Old Testament.
    A. The ark of the covenant.
    B. The day of expiation or atonement; Lev. 16.

Chapter 7: Of the Sacraments of Grace down to Abraham.
I. The sacraments of the first period.
    A. God's clothing Adam and Eve.
    B. The sacrifices.

II. The sacrament of the second period was the rainbow.
    A. This sacrament was not formally and precisely a sacrament of
       the covenant of grace.

B. The sacrament and covenant is only possible on the basis of a covenant of grace.

C. There is a confirmation and typical representation of the covenant of grace.

Chapter 8: Of Circumcision.

I. The divine institution of circumcision.
  A. Circumcision was first instituted to Abraham and his whole household; Gen. 17:11ff.
  B. Circumcision was for males only.
    1. Women are accounted in and with the men to be in the covenant.
    2. The reasons for a male-only sign.
       a. To teach that salvation is not dependent upon the sign.
       b. Signified the imperfection of the OT economy.
  C. Circumcision could be administered by anyone.
  D. Circumcision was to be performed on the eighth day from birth.

II. The necessity of circumcision.
  A. The refusal to circumcise would lead to excommunication; Gen. 17:14.
  B. This does not mean that infants dying uncircumcised after the eighth day perish.

III. The spiritual signification of circumcision.
  A. Principally a sign and seal of the covenant of God with Abraham; Gen. 17:11; Rom. 4:11.[9]
  B. Three lessons taught by circumcision.
    1. Our misery.
    2. Our redemption.
    3. Our returns of gratitude.

IV. The abrogation of circumcision.
  A. Circumcision was to be "an everlasting covenant" signifying to the end of that age or till the coming of the Messiah.

---

[9]Witsius writes, "Circumcision was the sign and seal of this covenant; so that all, who duly submitted to this, according to God's prescription, were solemnly declared by God himself to be partakers of the promises made to Abraham: and, at the same time openly avowed, that, by a lively faith, they received the promised Messiah, and expected from him blessings of every kind. And thus circumcision became to them a seal of the righteousness of faith, Rom. 4:11."

B. Reasons for the abrogation of circumcision in the New Covenant.
   1. It prefigured that which was to come; Col. 2:17.
   2. It was part of the wall of partition between Jews and Gentiles that has been abolished by Christ; Eph. 2:15; Gal. 5:6.
   3. It was bloody, thereby signifying that Christ had not yet come.
C. Circumcision was abrogated gradually.

Chapter 9: Of the Passover.

I. The name "Passover."
   A. This name is used because God, while he killed the first born of the Egyptians, passed over the doors of the Israelites; Ex. 12:13.
   B. This term has several usages.
      1. Can refer to the passing over the Israelites.
      2. Can refer to the lamb; Ex. 12:21; Luke 22:7.
      3. Can refer to the sacrifices along with the lamb; Deut. 16:2.
      4. Can refer to the week of festivities; Luke 22:1.

II. The time of the Passover; Lev. 13:5.
   A. The month is Abib or Nisan; Ex. 13:4; Neh. 2:1; Esth. 3:7.
   B. The day was the fourteenth.
   C. The time of day was between the two evenings.
      1. That is between noon and sunset.
      2. Josephus says between ninth hour till the eleventh, or 3:00-5:00 p.m.

III. The place of the Passover.
   A. First, in Egypt; Ex. 12:21.
   B. Second, in the wilderness of Sinai; Numb. 9:5.
   C. Then in the place of God's choosing (The Temple); Deut. 16:5-6.

IV. The minister of the Passover.
   A. The common people.
   B. The Levites.
   C. The priests.

V. The guests of the Passover.
   A. All true-born Israelites, if not excluded by legal uncleanness; Ex. 12:6,47.

B. Proselytes who were circumcised; Ex. 12:48.

C. Women partook of the Passover.

   1. All the congregation is commanded to partake.

   2. Note examples of women partaking in 1 Sam. 1:3-4; Lk. 2:41.

   3. Women partook of other sacrifices; Numb. 18:11.

   4. Testimony of Maimonides.

D. A second Passover was performed for those who missed the first due to various circumstances; Numb. 9:10-11.

VI. The rites of the Passover.

A. The appointment of the Passover sacrifice.

   1. A lamb or kid was to be used; Ex. 12:3.

   2. Oxen were not used though they were used for other sacrifices during the Passover festival; 2 Chron. 35:8-9.

   3. The lamb had to be without blemish, male, and of the first year; Ex. 12:5.

B. The lamb was prepared by setting it apart on the tenth day.

C. The lamb was to be killed and its blood sprinkled on the doorposts.

D. The lamb was to be roasted thoroughly; Ex. 12:9.

E. The Lamb was to be eaten.

   1. Guests were to be dressed to leave.

   2. Guests were to eat with shoes on their feet.

   3. They were to eat it with unleavened bread.

   4. They were not to break the bones of the lamb.

   5. Leftovers were to be burned.

F. Some of the laws or rites of the Passover were perpetual while others were used only once and in Egypt.

VII. The mystery or significance of the Passover.

A. The significance of the Passover peculiar to Israel.

   1. The salvation of their firstborn sons.

   2. The bitter herbs represented the bitter life under Pharaoh.

   3. The unleavened bread represented the bread of affliction in Egypt; Deut. 16:3.

   4. They were soon to leave Egypt.

B. The significance of the Passover to all believers in Christ.

   1. The person of Christ under the type of a lamb; John 1:29,36.

     a. Christ was to be taken from among his brethren; Deut. 18:15; Heb. 2:14-17.

     b. Christ was to be perfect; 1 Pet. 1:19.

      c. Christ was to be a male; Jer. 31:22.

  2. The sufferings of Christ.

     a. The manner of his sufferings.

        i. The lamb was to be killed by the whole congregation, likewise Christ; Luke 23:18.

        ii. The blood of the lamb was to be shed, likewise Christ; 1 Pet. 1:19.

        iii. The lamb was to be cooked thoroughly, likewise Christ's suffering was complete and sufficient.

        iv. The roasting signifies the burning of the divine wrath.

     b. The place of Christ's sufferings is the same; Luke 12:33; 18:31.

     c. Time of his sufferings is the same; Matt. 27:46,50.

     d. The fruits of his sacrifice.

        i. God spares all those whose consciences are sprinkled with the blood of Christ; Isa. 52:15; 1 Pet. 1:2; Heb. 12:24.

        ii. We are freed from bondage of Satan, the world, and sin; Heb. 2:14-15; John 8:36.

        iii. The salvation of the Gentiles as God judges the gods of the Egyptians; Numb. 33:4.

        iv. The Passover became the New Year and Christ introduced a new age.

  3. The manner in which we are made partakers of his sacrifice.

     a. We need to be sprinkled with the blood of Christ; Heb. 10:22.

     b. We need to partake (eat) of Christ; John 6:53.

     c. The bitter herbs reveal that we need to share with Christ in his sufferings; Phil. 3:10.

     d. The unleavened bread signifies that we need to separate ourselves from corruption and hypocrisy.

     e. We are to be sojourners in this life and be ready for action; 1 Pet. 1:3.

     f. We need to flee from sin and bondage.

     g. The lamb was to eaten in one house, out of which it was not lawful to go. This house is the church out of which there is no salvation, no communion with Christ.

Chapter 10: Of the extraordinary Sacraments in the Wilderness.

I. The passage in the cloud through the Red Sea.

A. The name of the Red Sea may have reference to Esau.
B. The events of the Red Sea were miraculous.
C. Exegesis of 1 Cor. 10:1-2.
   1. "Under the cloud" refers to near, not literally under.
   2. Meaning of "baptized in the cloud and in the sea."
      a. Uses baptism in a figurative sense.
      b. Similarities between cloud/sea and water.
      c. The sign of cloud and sea signify the same thing; 1 Pet. 3:21.
   3. Baptized unto Moses means by Moses.
D. The spiritual significance of the cloud.
   1. A symbol of God's gracious presence.
   2. It prefigured the future incarnation of the Son of God.
   3. It signified God's protection towards the elect.
   4. God in Christ takes on the evils that threaten his elect.
E. The spiritual significance of the passage through the Red Sea.
   1. Pharaoh and the Egyptians represent the devil and sin.
   2. Moses was a type of Christ, our deliverer and Savior.
   3. The waters signify afflictions and death itself.
   4. The east wind was an emblem of the Spirit of Christ.
   5. The Israelites are a figure of believers.

II. The sacrament of manna; 1 Cor. 10:3.
A. The name is derived from "he prepared, appointed, determined."
B. God used natural causes to make manna.
C. The origin of the manna was from God as the principal cause; Ex. 16:4,8,16; Deut. 8:3,16; Neh. 9:15,20,21.
D. The adjuncts of the manna.
   1. The internal adjuncts.
      a. The figure.
         i. Small.
         ii. Round.
         iii. Like coriander seed.
      b. Color was white.
      c. Taste.
         i. Like a wafer of honey; Ex. 16:31.
         ii. Like the taste of fresh oil; Numb. 11:8.
   2. The external adjuncts.
      a. The place was the wilderness.
      b. The time of the manna.
         i. None before the Exodus.

ii. Given when there was no other food.
iii. Given every day but the Sabbath.
iv. Given for forty years until they came to Canaan.
E. The duties with respect to the manna.
1. Gather early in the morning.
2. Gather it by a certain measure; a homer for each.
3. None of the manna was to last till the next day.
4. The day before the Sabbath they were to gather a double amount.
5. A homer of manna was to be placed near the Ark.
F. The sins of the Israelites with respect to the manna.
1. Some kept the manna till the next day.
2. Some looked for it on the Sabbath.
3. They disdained the manna.
G. The mystery or spiritual significance of the manna was that it represented Christ as the bread of heaven; John 6:32.

III. The water from the rock signified Christ as one who gives us life; 1 Cor. 10:4.

IV. The brazen serpent represented Christ; John 3:14.
A. The form of the serpent.
B. The matter of the serpent, i.e., bronze.
C. The lifting up of the serpent.
D. The benefit of the serpent.

Chapter 11: Of the Blessings of the Old Testament.
I. The election of the Israelites for a peculiar people; Deut. 7:6.
A. Israel was the "first born of God"; Ex. 4:22.
B. Israel was God's special treasure.
C. Israel was chosen to glory in God as their portion; Deut. 26:17.
D. The Messiah would be an Israelite; Deut. 16:15,18.

II. The land of Canaan.
A. The land of Canaan was promised to Abraham and his descendants; Gen. 12:7; 13:15; 15:7.
B. The land of Canaan was typical of our eternal inheritance.
1. Numb. 14:21,23 (Ps. 95:11); cf. with Heb. 4:11 where Paul refers to the eternal rest purchased by Christ implying the land of Canaan was typical.
2. The analogy or similitude of the land of Canaan consists in:

a. The land of Canaan was pleasant.
b. The land of Canaan was God's land; Hosea 9:3.
c. The land of Canaan was given in virtue of God's grace;
   Deut. 7:7-8; 4:37-38; Ez. 16:60; 36:32.
d. Joshua, not Moses (who represented law), brought
   them into the land of Canaan.

III. The demonstration of the divine majesty.
   A. Majesty revealed at Mt. Sinai; cf. Deut. 32-33.
   B. Majesty revealed in the pillar of cloud and fire; in the cloud in
      the temple, etc.

IV. The daily use of the various ceremonies.
   A. Christ was pictured in the ceremonial law.
   B. The godly found much comfort, delight, and learned much
      from the ceremonial law.
   C. This is not to deny that the ceremonial law was somewhat of a
      burden and part of the bondage of the Old Testament economy.

V. The almost uninterrupted succession of inspired prophets.
   A. The Israelites had men of God they could consult and learn
      the will of God.
   B. Moses was followed by a succession of prophets except some
      very few and short intervals; 1 Sam. 3:1; 2 Chron. 15:3.

Chapter 12: Of the Imperfections falsely ascribed to the Old Testament.
I. No true or permanent benefits of salvation in the Old Testament.
   A. Arguments in support of this position.
      1. Type and not truth in OT.
      2. Shadow of and not the permanent blessings in OT.
      3. Salvation not complete in OT; Heb. 2:3.
   B. Witsius answers.
      1. Christ bestowed on believers even under the Mosaic
         economy true benefits, in and with the typical.[10]
      2. A mutable economy in some respects does not imply
         mutable in all respects.
      3. Need to distinguish between salvation and the promise of
         salvation and not between salvation and temporal benefits.

[10]Witsius writes, "Did the types of the Israelites only prefigure that measure of grace,
peculiar to the New Testament; not saving grace itself which is common to both
dispensations? Were their sacraments signs only of this grace which is freely bestowed
on us, and not also of that of which they themselves were made partakers?"

Christ's promise was sufficient to bestow eternal salvation
on OT believers.

II. Circumcision of the heart or regeneration is a New Testament
blessing.
  A. Circumcision of the heart belongs to the covenant of grace
  and thus was in the Old Testament.
  B. Deut. 30:6 refers to a period within the OT.

III. The writing of the law on the heart is a NT blessing.
  A. OT saints had the law written on their hearts; Ps. 119:11,16,47.
  B. OT saints loved God without fear with exceeding joy, which
  assumes the writing of the law on their hearts.

IV. No proper forgiveness of sins in the Old Testament.
  A. The OT does express the forgiveness of sins; Ps. 130:4; 32; 103;
  51; Ex. 34:7; cf. Jam. 2:21; Rom. 4:2-3.
  B. Jesus forgave sins before He died on the cross; Matt. 9:2.
  C. The difference between the OT and NT.
    1. There are three things that are required for full
    forgiveness.
      a. The taking away of sin from the believer.
      b. The transferring upon Christ.
      c. The expiating of sin by Christ.
    2. The first two were a reality in the OT.

V. Adoption is a New Testament blessing.
  A. Adoption existed in the OT; Job 34:36; Isa. 63:16; cf. Gal. 4:4-7.
  B. The difference between the OT and NT.
    1. OT believers were considered and treated as young
    children and thus did not differ much from servants;
    Gal. 4:4-7.
    2. OT believers did not enjoy the full benefits and privileges
    of being children of God.

VI. Peace of conscience is a New Testament blessing; Heb. 10.
  A. The Scriptures affirm that OT believers had peace of
  conscience; Ps. 3:5; 4:3; 17:15.
  B. Their sin was forgiven which brought peace.
  C. Heb. 10 is misinterpreted.
    1. Imperfection is ascribed to the ceremonial law.

   2. The "consciousness of sin" of verse 2 is not their sin
       barring them from access to God but a consciousness of
       sin as not yet expiated.
 D. Believers did not have the peace that comes from the ransom
    being fully paid but they did have peace knowing that they did
    not have to pay it and that the Messiah would one day do so.

VII. OT believers were subject to the dominion of angels; Heb. 2:5.
 A. This is a misinterpretation of Heb. 2:5.
 B. Angels were ministering spirits.

VIII. OT believers were subject to the continual fear of temporal death.
 A. Arguments in favor of this position.
    1. They did not want to die so they could enjoy the Promised
        Land.
    2. They did not want to die so they could see the Messiah.
    3. The threat of death for disobedience; Heb. 2:15.
 B. Witsius answers:
    1. God did punish some with death; Lev. 24:16; Num. 15:34;
        Lev. 10:2; 1 Sam. 6:20; 2 Sam. 6:7-9. Yet His acts of fatherly
        kindness are much more conspicuous.
    2. The eternal inheritance was more precious to them than
        the typological one.
    3. Saints who pleaded with God for a longer life did so that
        they might glorify God; Psa. 6:4-5; Isa. 38:18-19.
    4. Not all had the hope of seeing the Messiah.
    5. They misinterpret Heb. 2:15.
        a. The benefit of Christ's death is for all the elect and not
            just those who lived in Canaan.
        b. The author is speaking of the pre-conversion state.
        c. The author is referring to temporal and eternal death.
        d. Paul speaks of those who were all their lifetime subject
            to the fear of death, yet OT saints went to heaven
            when they died.

IX. OT believers were under the wrath and curse of God.
 A. Arguments for their position.
    1. OT believers were under the curse; Gal. 3:10.
    2. OT believers were under a time of wrath and severity;
        Isa. 10:25; Dan. 8:19; 2 Cor. 3:7-9; Rom. 4:15,
 B. Witsius answers:
    1. With respect to the curse:

a. Paul is refuting the legalism of the Judaizers.

b. Paul is referring to the curse of the covenant of works.

2. With respect to the wrath and severity.

a. Isaiah and Daniel are not contrasting the covenants but that period of time that God more severely punishes his people, which he sometimes does in the NT.

b. Moses is called a minister of death because his ministry for the most part tended to terrify the sinner and convince him of his sin.

c. The law works wrath in the sense that it convinces man of his sin and raises in the soul a sense of wrath.

Chapter 13: Of the real defects of the Old Testament.

I. The cause of salvation was not completed.

A. The sins of the OT believers remained.

B. Their sins remained in Christ's account.

II. The obscurity of the OT economy.

III. Greater threatenings of the Law, lesser promises of grace; Heb. 12:18.

IV. Bondage to the ceremonial law; Gal. 4:3,9.

A. Bondage to the vast multitude of laws.

1. Laws, which could not make one perfect and had no elements of holiness in themselves.

2. Their mystical significance did point to Christ.

B. Bondage to laws suitable for children; Gal. 4:2.

C. The middle wall of partition secluding the Gentiles and familiar access to God; Eph. 2:14-15.

D. Ceremonial law contained an element of enmity.

1. Need to distinguish between legal and evangelical aspect.

2. Legal aspect contained enmity between God and Israel and Israel and the Gentiles.

E. There was a "hand-writing" in the religious ceremonies.

1. A confession of sin; deserved utter destruction; no salvation apart from satisfaction of divine justice by a substitute.

2. That this satisfaction was not yet accomplished.

V. The spirit of bondage.

A. The spirit of bondage is the work of the Holy Spirit in a manner suitable to the old economy.

B. The work of the spirit of bondage in OT.
   1. Taught that it was good to submit to the ceremonial laws.
   2. To seek the spiritual significance of the laws and not to cleave to the outward rite only.
   3. Inclined the wills of believers and taught them to long for the liberty of the new covenant.
C. The difference between the testaments with respect to bondage is that between a child and adult.

VI. A more scanty measure of the gifts of grace.
   A. With respect to extent.
      1. God only called the nation of Israel to be his people.
      2. In that one nation, very few were partakers of saving grace; 1 Cor. 10:5.
   B. With respect to degree in the following areas:
      1. The knowledge of spiritual mysteries.
      2. The abundance of spiritual consolations.
      3. Holiness which depends upon the above.
   C. The comparison of the measure of grace must be done according to category.
      1. We must compare church to church; prophets to apostles; ancient heroes to martyrs.
      2. There were the select few, who had large measures of grace.
      3. The church as a whole had a scanty measure of grace compared to the NT church as a whole.

VII. OT believers had a hunger and thirst for a better condition according to God's promise; John 8:56; Matt. 13:17; Heb. 11:13.

Chapter 14: Of the Abrogation of the Old Testament.
I. The ceremonial law could be abrogated.
   A. The ceremonial law was founded on the free and arbitrary will of God.
   B. God Himself prefers the moral over the ceremonial law; 1 Sam. 15:22; Isa. 1:11; Jer. 7:22.
   C. The OT church was at times destitute of the ceremonies.

II. The ceremonial law was abrogated.
   A. The ceremonial law was intended for Israel alone.
   B. The Scriptures foretold of their abrogation.
      1. In general their abrogation is foretold.

>   a. Deut. 18:15,18.
>   b. Jer. 31:31-34.
>   2. In particular their abrogation is foretold.
>   a. The ark; Jer. 3:16-17.
>   b. The Priesthood; Ps. 110:4; cf. Heb. 8:11-13.
>   c. The sacrifices; Dan. 9:27.

III. The ceremonial law ought, one time or other, to be abrogated.
    A. The inclusion of the Gentiles into the kingdom makes the ceremonial laws impossible to keep.
    B. The ceremonial laws are but shadows; a yoke to be broken.

IV. The stages of abrogation of the ceremonial law.
    A. The sign of their abrogation was the coming of Christ; John 4:21.
    B. The ceremonial law was abrogated in point of right by Christ's death.
    C. Abrogation was confirmed by the resurrection of Christ, his ascension and gift of the Holy Spirit.
    D. Their abrogation still needed to be taught; Acts 10:11.
    E. Church declaration of their abrogation; Acts 15.
    F. Paul preached their abrogation.
    G. Apostles' use of ceremonial law was to not offend the weaker brother and to win them to Christ; Acts 21:22.
    H. Paul accused Peter of falling back into the use of the ceremonies.
    I. The ceremonial law was finally abrogated at the destruction of Jerusalem.

Chapter 15: Of the Benefits of the New Testament.

I. The presence of the Messiah; 1 Tim. 1:15.

II. The gospel of the Kingdom as completed.

III. The calling of the Gentiles; Ps. 2:8; Isa. 49:6; Luke 2:40.
    A. Accomplished by the Apostles.
    B. The Gentiles responded quickly to the gospel.
    C. The call went to the ends of the earth.
    D. The gospel did not reach the Gentiles until it was first rejected by the Jews.
    E. Jews were not rejected until the kingdom was established among the Gentiles.

IV. A more abundant and delightful measure of the Spirit.

A. Foretold by the Prophets; Zech. 9:12; Isa. 44:2-3; 35:7; Joel 2:28.
B. The effects of the Spirit.
   1. A more clear and distinct knowledge of the mysteries of faith; Isa. 11:9; 54:13: Jer. 31:34; 1 John 2:27.
   2. A more generous, a more sublime and cheerful degree of holiness; Isa. 33:24; 35:9; 60:21-22; Zech. 10:5; 12:8.
   3. A more delightful consolation; Isa. 40:1-2; 60:1-2; 55:11; 66:12-14; John 14:16; Acts 9:31; Eph. 1:13; 2 Cor. 1:22.
   4. A filial boldness, which is now greater, as adoption itself, and its effects are more conspicuous; Gal. 4:6.
   5. The gifts of the Spirit; Mk. 16:16-18; Acts 10:45-46; 19:6; 21:8; 1 Cor. 12:7-11.

V. Christian liberty.
   A. Liberty common to all believers.
      1. From the tyranny of the devil.
      2. From the reigning and condemning power of sin.
      3. From the rigour of the law.
      4. From death.
      5. From the laws of men.
      6. From the obligations to things indifferent.
   B. Liberty common to NT believers.
      1. From the ceremonial laws.
      2. From things indifferent in their own nature, the use of, or abstinence from, which formerly enjoined the Israelites; Tit. 1:15; Col. 2:20-21; 1 Cor. 10:25.
      3. The judicial laws that were particular to Israel.
      4. A clear and more perfect knowledge and practice of Christian liberty.

VI. The restoration of Israel.
   A. Exegesis of Rom. 11:25-27.
      1. Paul is explaining a mystery.
      2. The interest of Gentiles is involved.
      3. Paul speaks of literal Israel.
      4. Israel is considered as a nation from beginning to end and a part of it has now been hardened.
      5. The hardening will continue until the fullness of the Gentiles come into the kingdom.
      6. All Israel (nation as a whole) will be saved when the fullness of the Gentiles have come.

  B. "All Israel" does not refer to mystical Israel but to the Jewish nation.
1. In verses 1 and 14, Paul refers them to his own pedigree, calls them his own flesh and kindred, and distinguishes them from the Gentiles.
2. Paul is dealing with a mystery but it is no mystery that Jews were converted with the Gentiles.
3. Purpose is to deflate the pride of the Gentiles.
4. The falling away is to be joined with their restoration.
5. Paul refers to Isa. 61:20
  C. Further Scriptural support; Lev. 26:41-45; Deut. 4:30-31; 30:1-6; 32:43; Psa. 102:14-18; 85:9-10; Isa. 11:11-12; 19:24-25; 49:14ff; 62; Jer. 3:18ff; 33:24-26; Ez. 36:24ff; 37:15; 34:25ff.; Hosea 13:29; Luke 21:24; 2 Cor. 3:16.

VII. The riches of the whole church.
  A. This will occur after and due to the restoration of Israel.
  B. Riches will be greater with respect to degree and extent.

Chapter 16: Of Baptism.

I. Two-fold baptism use by the Jews.
  A. The baptism of uncleanness.
  B. The baptism of Proselytism.

II. Divine institutions of baptism.
  A. John's baptism; Luke 3:2; John 1:33.
  B. Christian baptism.
  C. The similarities between the two baptisms.
    1. Both based on God's command.
    2. Both involved water.
    3. Both administered into faith and confession of Christ.
    4. Both a sign and seal of the remission of sins.
    5. Both involve an obligation to repentance.
  D. The differences between the two baptisms.
    1. John's baptism was from God but not from Christ as the mediator.
    2. John's baptism was a preparation, introduction, or initiation for Christian baptism.
    3. God communicated a more sparing measure of the Spirit in John's baptism.

III. Christian baptism.
   A. The mode of baptism.
      1. Arguments for immersion.
         a. Christ and the Apostles used this mode as seen by the example of the ancient church.
         b. "Baptize" often refers to immersion.
         c. A fuller similitude between the sign and the thing signified.
      2. Arguments for pouring or sprinkling.
         a. Example of the three thousand (Acts 2:41) in one day and of Cornelius, Lydia, and the jailer exclude the possibility of immersion.
         b. "Baptize" can refer to sprinkling or pouring.
         c. The thing signified by baptism is explained in the OT and NT in terms of sprinkling and pouring; Isa. 52:15; Ez. 36:25; Heb. 12:24; 1 Pet. 1:2; Heb. 9:13-14.
   B. The manner of baptism.
      1. Immersing or sprinkling once or three times is indifferent.
      2. Words of explanation are to accompany baptism.[11]
      3. It is to be done in the name of the Triune God.
   C. The spiritual meaning of baptism.
      1. The general meaning.
         a. Communion with Christ and his body along with all his benefits; 1 Cor. 12:13; Tit. 3:5; 1 Pet. 3:21.
         b. An engagement to incumbent duty; 1 Pet. 3:21.
      2. The particular meaning.
         a. Water signifies the blood as the impetrating cause (Heb. 12:24; 1 Pet. 1:2), and the Spirit as the applying cause (Isa. 44:3; Ez. 36:25-27).
         b. Signifies both present and future benefits received from union with Christ.
         c. Signifies the putting off of sin (1 Pet. 3:21), and the putting on of Christ (Gal. 3:26-27).
         d. Signifies our duty towards God (Matt. 28:19-20); ourselves (Rom. 6:3-6); our brother (1 Cor. 12:13; Eph. 4:3,5).
   D. The role of the Trinity in baptism.
      1. Father promises salvation.
      2. Son obtains salvation as mediator.
      3. Spirit applies salvation.

---

[11]Witsius quotes Augustine, "Take away the word, and what is the water but the water only?"

E. Children of believers are to be baptized.
  1. Children of believers in the OT were to receive the sign of the covenant; Gen. 17.
  2. Peter speaks of the inclusion of children in the covenant in the NT; Acts 2:38-39; as does Christ; Matt. 16:13-15; Luke 18:15.
  3. Children of believers are called "holy"; 1 Cor. 7:14.
  4. Those who belong to the church of God have a right to baptism.
  5. Baptism took the place of circumcision; Col. 2:11-12.

Chapter 17: Of the Lord's Supper.

I. The elements of the Lord's Supper.
  A. The elements are bread and wine.
    1. Enables the sacrament to be enjoyed universally.
    2. Consistent with the NT economy.
    3. Not a bloody sacrament.
  B. Unleavened bread should be used.
  C. Wine should be used.
    1. Red is preferable but not necessary.
    2. Not necessary to mix wine with water.
  D. Other elements may be used in extreme situations rather than depriving God's people of this sacrament.

II. The actions of the Lord's Supper.
  A. Christ's actions with respect to the bread.
    1. He took it.
    2. He blessed it.
    3. He broke it.
    4. He gave it.
  B. Christ's words with respect to the bread.
    1. Preceptive: Take, eat, do this in remembrance of me.
    2. Explicatory: This is my body, which is given for you.
  C. Christ's actions with respect to the cup.
    1. He took the cup.
    2. He gave thanks.
    3. He gave it.
  D. Christ's words with respect to the cup.
    1. Preceptive: Drink ye all of it, in remembrance of me.
    2. Explicatory: This is the blood of the new covenant, which is shed for the remission of sins.

    E. Actions of the disciples.
       1. Received both bread and the cup.
       2. Ate the bread and drank the cup.

III. The recipients of the Lord's Supper.
    A. The necessary requirements.
       1. A knowledge of the faith; able to discern the Lord's body; and understand the analogy of the sacrament and thereby can show the Lord's death until he comes.
       2. A repentant and believing heart.
    B. Infants are therefore excluded from the Lord's Supper.

IV. When to celebrate the Lord's Supper.
    A. Christ does not give a specific number since he says "as often."
    B. A moderate or balanced approach should be taken.

V. The spiritual meaning of the Lord's Supper.
    A. A sign for our instruction.
       1. Bread signifies the body of Christ.
       2. Wine signifies the blood of Christ.
       3. The taking of the element sets forth Christ to believers.
       4. The breaking of the bread represents Christ's death.
       5. The pouring of the wine represents his shed blood.
       6. The receiving of the elements signifies their receiving Christ.
       7. The eating and drinking of the elements.
          a. Meditating upon Christ.
          b. Communion with Christ.
    B. A seal, ratifying to us the promises and grace of God.
       1. Present blessings.
          a. Union and communion with Christ
          b. Conservation and sanctification.
          c. Satisfaction and delight in God.
       2. Future blessings of the life to come.
    C. A solemn engagement to our duty to Christ.
       1. To keep our duty of a chaste, faithful, and loving spouse.
       2. To reciprocate the love of Christ exhibited in the Supper.
       3. To remember Christ's death on our behalf.
       4. To receive Christ's communion with us; Rev. 3:20.
    D. A solemn engagement to our duty to our brother in the Lord.